FOR OFFICIAL USE ONLY

HISTORY OF THE GREAT WAR

BASED FROM OFFICIAL DOCUMENTS
BY DIRECTION OF THE HISTORICAL SECTION
OF THE
WAR CABINET SECRETARIAT

THE OCCUPATION OF CONSTANTINOPLE 1918-1923 (Provisional)

COMPILED BY
Brigadier-General SIR JAMES E. EDMONDS
C.B., C.M.G., Hon. D. Litt. (Oxon), R.E. (retired), p.s.c.

Transcribed by Neil Wells

Crown Copyright Reserved

The Naval & Military Press Ltd

Published by
The Naval & Military Press Ltd
5 Riverside, Brambleside, Bellbrook
Industrial Estate, Uckfield, East Sussex,
TN22 1QQ England
Tel: +44 (0) 1825 749494
Fax: +44 (0) 1825 765701

www.naval-military-press.com
www.military-genealogy.com
www.militarymaproom.com

Copyright © The Naval and Military Press Ltd 2010

PREFACE

Originally when the British official historian Sir James Edmonds was planning the official history series he foresaw two volumes covering the post war occupations of former enemy states namely Germany and Turkey. However, due to Foreign Office objections relating to the possible unlawful actions concerning the occupations, the writing of them was put on hold. Even without the permission to publish, the research for these volumes was still conducted by Edmonds in the 1930's. Interest in the occupation of Germany was revived in 1942 at what was seen to be the turning point of the Second World War and an invasion of mainland Europe possible in the near future. Therefore the decision was taken to write the German occupation book. Edmonds decided to write both 'occupation' volumes in 1943 even though only the German volume, which was titled 'The Occupation of the Rhineland 1918-1929', was sanctioned. This volume was published in 1944.

This book, the second occupation volume, was written during the summer of 1944. On the completion of the draft manuscript, it was stored within the Public Records Office, London. The British Official History set, therefore remains, incomplete to this day.[1]

The typed copy of the draft manuscript that I used in producing this book has been reproduced word for word and not edited in any way. However, the copy was not of good quality and in a couple of places, small parts of the original text were either missing or were unreadable. In such cases, to complete the text, I have taken an educated guess at what the original text was; in those cases I have used italics to show that it is my interpretation. Therefore if there is any misinterpretation of any of the above 'missing texts', I take full responsibility. In the draft manuscript an additional appendix was added, giving two appendix I (the second one located between appendices II and III which seem to be appropriate). I therefore renamed appendix II to IIa and the second appendix I to IIb and listed them both as such within the List of Appendices. The full title was given for each of the appendices in the Table of Appendices whilst an abbreviated title was given at the top of each appendix. I have used the full title.

The British Official Histories were illustrated with maps and in some cases diagrams and photographs. To illustrate this volume I have used two officially published maps from the 1920's and photographs from the Imperial War Museum, Photographic Archive. I therefore thank The Keeper and his staff of the archive for the use of the photographs.

Finally place names are shown as they were, however some have be renamed. The most important of these are: Constantinople, which is now known as Istanbul, Smyrna is now Izmir and Adrianople is now Edirne.

N.J.W.
London, 14th April 2009

---

[1] In the British Officials series, apart from this volume, which was written but not published, the second volume of the Military Operations, East Africa, is missing. It was intended to write and publish it, and indeed a couple of draft chapters were written, but due to the death of its author, Lieutenant Colonel Charles Norden, it was not completed. These draft chapters are now stored at the P.R.O., London.

NOTE

The war diaries for the period are far from complete. The British General Staff diaries stop at the end of October 1920 and their reports stop at the end of July 1922. No A. & Q. diaries can be found after September 1922(?) and their reports which are available contain little except the daily weather reports, men reporting sick, and the number of men proceeding home on being demobilized, or going on leave. The diaries of the 26th Division, the principle formation concerned, cease after November 1920 and there are no R.A. or R.E. diaries at all for 1920. The official files of G.H.Q. Constantinople, and the War Office files were available, also the records of the Commissions of Control and Organization and the printed procès-verbaux of the "Directing Committee of Generals." General Sir George Milne's Report, dated 11th August 1920, was found to be a valuable guide. Only extracts of the reports of the British High Commissioner, sent by the Foreign Office to the War Office, were available.

In the spelling of Turkish place names, English custom at the time has been followed, except that Angora has been abandoned in favour of Ankara. It was thought that Smyra, Brusa, Gallipoli, Chanak, etc., might not be recognized in Iamir, Bursa, Gellibolu, Canak, etc., which now appear in official handbooks.

This compilation was put together in some haste. Any corrections and additions thought desirable should be sent to the Secretary, Historical Section, War Cabinet Secretariat, S.W.1.

J.E.E.
Historical Section, War Cabinet Secretariat,
27th September 1944.

CONTENTS

The Armistice: Occupation of the Straits and Batum: G.H.Q. and the High Commissioners at Constantinople: Effective Occupation of Constantinople: Inter-Allied Police Commission: Execution of the Armistice Terms: Turkish Demobilization and Handing Over of Arms: Rise of the Nationalists Movement: Formal Occupation of Constantinople: The Unratified Peace Treaty of Sèvres: The Tripartite Agreement: The Strength of the Allied Army of Occupation: Orders for the Reduction of the British Contingent: The New Organization of the International Force: General Harington Arrives to take Command: Change in the Situation: King Constantine Returns: Allied Differences over Command: The Sub-Commissions: The Directing Committee of Generals: The Many Commissions: Formation of the Sub-Commissions: The Inter-Allied Liaison Section: The Turkish-Greek Struggle: Greek Threat to Constantinople: Defeat of the Greeks in Anatolia: Defence of the Dardanelles: Chanak: The Mudania Convention: The Peace Treaty of Lausanne: Evacuation.

TABLE OF APPENDICES

Appendix I: The Terms of the Armistice with Turkey, 30th October, 1918	36
Appendix IIa: The Military Inter-Allied Commission of Control and Organization	39
Appendix IIb: Composition and Location of the Military Inter-Allied Commission of Control and Organization	41
Appendix III: Tripartite Agreement between the British Empire, France and Italy Respecting Anatolia signed at Sèvres 10th August, 1920	43
Appendix IV: The Military, Naval and Air Clauses of the Treaty of Peace with Turkey, signed at Sèvres 10th August, 1920 (Unratified)	44
Appendix V: Order by Lieut.-General Sir Charles Harington, Commanding-in-Force, Allied Forces of Occupation on Jurisdiction and Maintenance of Law and Order in Constantinople, 8th September, 1921	48
Appendix VI: Army of the Black Sea: Statistics of Order of Battle, September, 1920	50

PHOTOGRAPHS
(Between pages 29 & 30)

General View of Constantinople, 18 March 1920. (IWM Q37441)

Constantinople from HMS Montrose 5 December 1919. (IWM Q37431)

The 28th Division landing at Constantinople with French Sailors looking on, November 1918. (IWM Q13870)

The 28th Division marching through the Streets of Constantinople, November 1918 (IWM Q13874)

Lieut.-General Sir Henry Maitland Wilson taking the Salute, Constantinople, 10 Novmber 1918 (IWM Q13864)

Released British Prisoners of War about to be Repatriated, November 1918, Constantinople (IWM Q13949)

General Franchet d'Esperey coming Ashore, Constantinople, 8 February 1919 (IWM Q13946)

General Franchet d'Esperey, with General Sir George Milne behind, taking the Salute, Constantinople, 8 February 1919. (IWM Q13947)

Round Up of Turkish Officials being guarded by the Royal Navy, Constantinople, (IWM Q113471)

The Entrance of the Arsenal, Constantinople, c1919. (IWM Q14269)

Interior of the Arsenal, Constantinople, c1919. Note the stacks of Rifles. (IWM Q14268)

General Sir Edmund Ironside (centre) and Staff, Constantinople, c1920. (IWM Q113473)

MAPS

Map 1. The Mediterranean Theatre (Copy from Official History of the War – Military Operations, Gallipoli Volume I: Inception of the Campaign to May 1915. - Appendices & Maps Volume). 31

Map 2. Turkey in Europe – Zone of the Straits – Smyrna – The Islands (Copy from Treaty of Peace Between the Allied and Associated Powers and Turkey. (Treaty Series No. 10 (1920)) [Cmd. 964]). 32

LIST OF BOOKS ETC.,
TO WHICH MOST FREQUENT REFERENCE IS MADE

Alarums and Excursions.
Lieut.-General G. T. M. Bridges.

The Occupation of the Rhineland 1918-29.
Brig.-General Sir James E. Edmonds. H.M.S.O. 1944

Tim Harington Looks Back.
Lieut.-General Sir Charles H. (Tim) Harington.

With the British Army in Constantinople. A Personal Narrative.
(*Army Quarterly*, July and October 1933). Major-General Sir Thomas Marden

CALENDAR OF PRINCPLE EVENTS

1918

October

13 Turkish Government request good offices of President Wilson to re-establish peace.
20 Major-General Sir C. Townshend reaches Mitylene with Turkish peace offer.
26 Turkish representative reach Mudros.
30 Armistice signed.

November

10-11 Dardanelles defences occupied by troops of 28th Division.
11 Armistice between the Allies and Germany signed.
13 Lieut.-General Sir H. Maitland Wilson arrives in Constantinople as Commander of the Allied Corps.
14 Bosphorus defences occupied, 3/Middlesex arrives in Constantinople.

December

8 Turkish Government requested to disarm civil population of Constantinople.
17 General Milne's Headquarters as Commander of the Allied Army of the Black Sea established at Constantinople.
19 27th Division from Salonika reaches Constantinople on its way to Batum.

1919

January

11 General Milne instructed to assume executive control of Constantinople police.

February

8 General Franchet d'Espérey establishes his headquarters in Constantinople as Allied C. -in-C. Armées allées en Orient.

March

– 22nd Division demobilized at Salonika.

May

– 26th Division demobilized at Salonika.
15 Greek troops land and occupy Smyrna

CALENDAR OF PRINCPLE EVENTS

August
7   Nationalist Congress at Erzeroum meets.
15   Withdrawal of 27th Division from the Caucasus begins.

September
–   27th Division demobilized.

October
20   First measures taken to be prepared against Nationalist attack.
28   The French 122nd Division removed from Allied Corps.
–   Soviet-Turkish Agreement.
–   General Election in Turkey won by Nationalists.

1920

January
28   Nationalists raid arms from a Dardanelles fort garrisoned by the French.

March
16   Constantinople occupied by the Allies.

April
–   French defeated in Cilicia by Nationalists.

May
11   Draft treaty handed to the Turks.

June
10   Constantinople garrison disarmed.
14   International force withdrawn from Batum.
–   Nationalists attack Ismid lines.

July
8   Greek troops enter Brusa.
25   Greek troops enter Adrianople.

August
10   Treaty of Sèvres signed.

September
25   Greek division takes over Ismid lines.

CALENDAR OF PRINCPLE EVENTS

29 Reduction of the Army of the Black Sea ordered.

October
10 General Bridge's mission abolished.
30 Allied Corps broken up.
—   General Harington arrives in Constantinople in relief of General Milne.

November
1   Sir Horace Rumbold appointed Ambassador to Turkey and High Commissioner.
8   Major-General T. Marden takes command of 28th Division.

December
a. King Constantine returns to Athens.

1921

February
—   Directing Committee of Generals formed.
21 Conference to revise Treaty of Sèvres meets.

July
8   Greeks begin campaign to reach Ankara.

September
13-20 Sub-commissions of Control formed.

November
17 Commission of Control and Organization officially formed.

1922

March
—   Paris Conference fails to arrange terms between Turks and Greeks.

July
—   Greek troops advance towards Constantinople.

August
26 Nationalists offensive against Greeks in Asia Minor begins.

CALENDAR OF PRINCPLE EVENTS

September
9   First Nationalists threat to Chanak.
18   Greek army expelled from Asia Minor by the Nationalists.

October
3   Mudania Conference meets.
8   Mudania Agreement signed.

November
20   Lausanne Conference meets.

1923

July
24   Treaty of Lausanne signed.

August
24   Treaty of Lausanne ratified.

October
2   Last British troops leave Constantinople.

THE OCCUPATION OF CONSTANTINOPLE 1918-1923
(PROVISIONAL)

THE ARMISTICE

On the 30th September, 1918 an armistice between the Entente Powers and Bulgaria was signed at Salonika. At that date the Turkish Armies, both in Palestine and in Mesopotamia, were in disorder and in difficulties: it is only necessary to mention that, on 1st October, Damascus was entered by British and Arab troops, and that on the Tigris a force of less than ten thousand Turks was preparing to make its last stand against four and a half British and Indian divisions. It was expected in London that Turkey would make peace proposals early in October. On the 4th October it was learnt on good authority that the Turkish Government had telegraphed to Berlin that it was about to ask for peace, as the Central Powers, as in the case of Bulgaria, had withdrawn so much of their assistance that it was no longer adequate, and the final great Entente offensive by American, French, British and Belgian troops on the whole of the active Western Front, begun on the 26th September, made it clear that no more help was likely to be forthcoming. In the next few days Turkish emissaries attempted to open peace negotiations through the British diplomatic representatives in Greece and Switzerland; but these emissaries were not accredited, and nothing could be gained by irregular discussions, it was decided to await a formal approach. The terms of an armistice had already been drafted in London and, with a few amendments, they were approved in Versailles on 7th October by a Conference of the Prime Ministers of Great Britain, France and Italy. It was also settled then that the terms of peace could be discussed only at the end of the war. Next day it became known that the pro-German Turkish Cabinet, in which Talaat Pasha was Grand Vizier and Enver Pasha Minister of War, had resigned, and that the new Turkish Government was about to inform the President of the United States of America of its desire to negotiate for peace.

On 13th October the Turkish Chargé d'affaires at Madrid requested the Spanish Government to ask the President of the United States to take upon himself the task of re-establishing peace. Before President Wilson could ascertain the wishes of all the Allies a further Turkish offer of peace was received, conveyed by Major-General Sir Charles Townshend, taken prisoner at Kut, who was released for the purpose and arrived at Mitylene on the 20th October.

Next day, the British Naval Commander-in-Chief in the Mediterranean, Vice-Admiral Hon. Sir Somerset A. Gough-Calthorpe, was informed from London that Major-General Townshend's message had been considered by H.M. Government and that they were ready at once to consider the conditions of an armistice and prepared in due course to consider terms of peace, but these could not be settled by Great Britain without consultation with her Allies, which would take time. The Naval Commander-in-Chief was also to inform the Turkish Government that he was authorized to receive a representative accredited by them to arrange the terms of an armistice. This invitation was accepted, and the Turkish representative reached Mudros, Lemnos, on 26th October.

In view of the change of conditions about to take place, the War Office sent out a British Mission, under Lieut.-General G.T.M. Bridges, to act as the official channel of communication between General Franchet d'Espérey, Commander of the Allied Armies in the Orient, and General Milne Commander-in-Chief of the British Salonika Army under him, neither of whom desired an intermediary. He was, in addition, to keep the War Office informed of all operations and intelligence affecting the Balkan theatre of war as a whole. He arrived at Salonika on 29th October.

On the 30th October, after five days' discussion, the terms of an armistice between the Turkish Government were agreed upon and signed upon on board *H.M.S. Agamemnon* at Port Mudros by Vice-Admiral Gough-Calthorpe, duly empowered on behalf of the Allies; in accordance with Article 24, hostilities ceased at noon, local time, on the next day.[1] It was subsequently regretted that the senior French admiral had not been asked to attach his signature to the Convention.

Nothing was said in the Articles as regards the duration or denunciation of the Armistice, or as regards any line of demarcation, or as regards any means of ensuring that the terms were being carried out, probably because the Turkish Army was in a state of dissolution; but certain securities were taken. Subsequently Vice-Admiral Gough-Calthorpe was appointed High Commissioner at Constantinople, his mission being confined to question affecting the execution of the Armistice terms and to the protection of British interests; the British commanders, General Sir Edmund Allenby in Syria, General Francis Wingate in the Hedjaz and General Sir William Marshall in Mesopotamia, were to continue to deal with matters in their own spheres.

The principal provisions of the terms of the Armistice were the immediate demobilization of the Turkish Army, except for such troops as were required for surveillance of frontiers and for the maintenance of internal order, the total and distribution of which was to be determined by the Allies (Article 5); the compliance with such orders as the Allies might give for the disposal of equipment, arms and ammunition, including transport, of the demobilized portion of the Turkish Army (Article 20); the Allied occupation of the Dardanelles and Bosphorus forts (Article 1); the right to occupy any strategic points if a situation arose which threatened the security of the Allies (Article 7); in case of disorder in the Armenian vilayets, the Allies reserved the right to occupy them (Article 24) – which would seem to preclude any idea of a general occupation; wireless telegraphs and cable stations were to be controlled by the Allies (Article 12); Allied control officers were to be placed on all railways, which were to be at the free and complete disposal of the Allies authorities (Article 15); and an Allied representative was to be attached to the Turkish Ministry of Supplies in order to order to safeguard Allied interests.

---

[1] In Appendix I the terms of the Armistice are given in full.

OCCUPATION OF THE STRAITS AND BATUM

After several changes of plan, it had been settled at the Conference of the Prime Ministers of Great Britain, France and Italy in Versailles on the 7th October, that the wing of the Allied Armies at Salonika destined to march on Constantinople should be under the immediate command of a British general, the other wing, under a French general, going to the Danube. Both generals, however, were to remain under the orders of General Franchet d'Espérey. It was also agreed that the Constantinople wing should consist mainly of British troops, but should include French, Italian, Serbian and Greek detachments.

At the hour of the Armistice coming into force the Army under General Milne's command consisted of three British,[1] one French and three Greek divisions, with Italian and Serbian detachments. This Army was 140 miles from Constantinople, and was preparing to force the passage of the Maritsa, which river, after passing through Adrianople (Turkish), then formed the Bulgarian-Turkish boundary down to the coast of the Ægean Sea, east of Dede Agach. On the right, under Lieut.-General Sir Henry F. Maitland Wilson, was the British 22nd Division (Major-General J. Duncan) at Dede Agach; the cavalry brigade was just north again was the French 122nd Division (General Topart); on the left was the British 26th Division (Major-General A.W. Gay); the Greek I. Corps of three divisions was in Greece, a hundred miles or more in rear; and the British 28th Division near Salonika.

To occupy the Turkish defences of the Dardanelles and the Bosphorus, General Milne proposed to send the infantry of one division by water from Dede Agach, and, on informing General Franchet d'Espérey of this, the latter replied that he would send a French regiment at the same time. In reporting the situation to the War Office, General Milne urged that a British General responsible only to his own Government should be immediately appointed to supervise the execution of the Armistice terms and to regularize the demands of the Allies. After communicating with Paris, General Franchet d'Espérey on instructions received, ordered one regiment of the French 122nd Division (which was under General Milne) to concentrate at Dede Agach for shipment through the Dardanelles, and for the remainder of the division to be transported by rail to Stambul; but Lieut.-General Maitland Wilson, commander of the XII. Corps, was appointed to the tactical command of the occupying force, as "G.O.C. Allies Forces, Gallipoli and Bosphorus"[2], and he was informed by G.H.Q. that he was appointed to be "the military channel of communication with the Turkish Government"[3].

The movement on Constantinople as planned could not take place, as Dede Agach, being exposed to the weather, proved an unsatisfactory port. The British 28th Division was therefore sent by General Milne direct from Salonika by sea, the 22nd Division was withdrawn by rail and road from Dede Agach to Macedonia, and the 26th Division, on the railway at Mustapha Pasha, joined the Army of the Daube in place of the 27th which had been held up by heavy snow storms and had returned to Macedonia.

General Franchet d'Espérey had intended that the British should occupy the Dardanelles, and the French the Bosphorus. This plan was cancelled by a decision of the two Governments, by which both nations were to participate in the occupation of both straits, command in the former being exercised by the British and in the latter by the French, the commanders of both,

---

[1] His fourth division was with the Army of the Danube. Five Indian battalions had just arrived at Salonika, and were attached singly to brigades of the 22nd and 28th Divisions.
[2] He signed as "Commanding the Allied Corps, Constantinople".
[3] He corresponded not only with the Minister of War, but also with the Foreign Ministry.

however, being under the orders of General Wilson.

The 28th Division (less artillery and wheeled transport, which followed later), under Major-General H. L. Croker, began embarking at Salonika on the 7th November; on the 9th the Turkish Minister of War was informed of the move to occupy the Dardanelles and Bosphorus defences; on the 10th and 11th, the latter being the day on which the Armistice with Germany was signed, as the French 122nd Division had not appeared, the 83rd and 84th Brigades landed without incident on both shores of the Dardanelles; and on the 12th the Allied fleet steamed through. When, on the 14th, the 85th Brigade arrived, it took over the defences on both shores of the Bosphorus, leaving one battalion, the 3/Middlesex, at Constantinople – it marched to Pera quarter – to provide guards in the city. The occupation of the capital had not been mentioned in the Armistice, but it might be regarded as one of the strategic points referred to in Article 7. Actually, the occupation amounted to no more than a partial one for the purpose of keeping order. The Ottoman Government did consider protesting at the size of the force, and went so far as to say that its arrival was tantamount to occupation; but when informed that it was merely the British G.H.Q., they were so taken aback that they said nothing further. Complete calm reigned in the population of 1,300,000, a few Turkish troops were to be seen; the nine thousand Germans and about a thousand Austrian troops in the city, General Liman von Sanders with them, obeyed orders to remove themselves to Haidar Pasha (a suburb of Constantinople on the Asiatic shore, the terminus of the Anatolian railway) without demur.[1] The local Government, the Sultan still being in his Bosphorus villa, and the officers of State in their offices were left to carry on as usual.

A few days later the French division arrived and began to take over, and by the 26th the distribution in the Dardanelles, under Major-General Croker, with Headquarters at Chanak, was: the 83rd Brigade held the Asiatic forts and the French 45th Regiment (of 3 battalions, like a British brigade), the European, with the 84th Brigade in reserve on the Gallipoli Peninsula. On the Bosphorus, under Colonel de Langlade of the French 84th Regiment, one battalion of the 85th Brigade held the European forts, and one battalion of the French 84th Regiment, the Asiatic; the remaining troops of the two Allied formations were distributed on both shores, with battalions in Pera, Stambul and Haidar Pasha. The French 148th Regiment was in reserve about San Stefano, west of Stambul.

Early in March, 1919 an Italian battalion, III/62nd Regiment, arrived and was stationed in Pera. It was followed by its two other battalions. The Greeks provided only guards for their Embassy and Consulate.

Lieut.-General Maitland Wilson, who had sailed with the fleet, accompanied by a French representative, General Bunoust, landed at Constantinople on 13th November, and took over command, with headquarters in the English Girls School, Gande Rue, Pera. He and his staff were lodged in the Pera Palace Hotel, and other officers in the London Hotel, Pera, which was taken over.

Fraternization was forbidden, and on the 14th November General Maitland Wilson issued the following order:

> "In view of special mentality of ruling classes, British Government consider it probable that Turkish propaganda may take form of attempting to secure sympathies of senior British officers. You will therefore issue strict orders that all offers of Turkish

---

[1] They were then disarmed and interned, the officers on Prince's Island and other ranks in a camp near Scutari (also on the Asiatic shore opposite Constantinople) until ships could be spared to repatriate them.

FRATERNIZATION

hospitality are to be refused pending the conclusion of Peace, and that relations between Allied Forces and Turkey should be limited to strictly official character. Admiralty have been asked to send similar telegram. Foreign Office is being asked to approach French Government on same lines."

On the 29th General Maitland Wilson had to warn the Turkish Foreign Minister that failure to give orders to the Turkish G.O.C. opposite General Allenby in Syria as to movement, demobilization and surrender of arms, and procrastination in Cicilia and Medina would not be tolerated. A conciliatory reply was received, but orders for the occupation of Constantinople as sanction and in case of civil disturbance were prepared. General Maitland Wilson also asked for the withdrawal of all Turkish troops in the Gallipoli Peninsula to North Bulair Lines by a fixed date.

On the 8th December the Turkish Government was requested by Lieut.-General Maitland Wilson to disarm the civil population of Constantinople.

British troops from the Mesopotamia Expeditionary Force were at this time at Baku, on the Caspian, for the purpose of preventing the Turks from gaining possession of the oil wells; and the Turks were still fighting White Russians and Armenians in the Caucasus, and had to be disarmed and turned out of the country; so in December it was decided in London to send the 27th Division (Major-General Sir George Forestier-Walker)[1] of the Salonika force to Batum, to form a link between Constantinople and Baku, and reopen the oil pipe line across Caucasia from Baku to Batum. The division began to arrive in Constantinople in the middle of December, and the leading brigade reached Batum on the 22nd.[2]

---

[1] On 9th March following he was invalided, and was succeeded in command by Major-General (Sir George) Cory, who had been General Milne's chief General Staff officer, in which capacity he succeeded by Major-General (Sir John) Duncan, commanding the 22nd Division, about to be demobilized.

[2] The other two Salonika divisions, the 22nd and 26th, were demobilized in March and May, respectively, the former after transferring three Battalions (9/King's Own, 9/East Lancashire and 9/South Lancashire) to the 28th Division.

An account of demobilization and the substitution in the units retained of young soldiers for war veterans will be found in "The Occupation of the Rhineland 1918-29", pp. 92, 93, 145. To augment the falling numbers, Indian battalion were brought to Constantinople, the 28th Division having 3 in April, 1919 and 8 in April, 1920. For a considerable time the infantry brigades consisted of one British and three Indian battalions.

G.H.Q AND THE HIGH COMMISSIONERS AT CONSTANTINOPLE

General Sir George Milne arrived at Constantinople on 17th December from Salonika, and established G.H.Q. in the Military School, Pera, from which date the troops under his command became known as the Army of the Black Sea, although the name was not officially assumed until the 13th May, 1919.

General Franchet d'Espérey arrived on the 23rd, but only on a visit; he did not make his formal entry until the 8th February, and then took possession of Enver Pasha's palace at Ortakeui, on the Bosphorus. Practically, he was excluded from command in Constantinople, and perhaps on a hint from Maréchal Foch, he made no protest, and was most punctilious in his behaviour, sending orders for the movement of French troops in Constantinople through General Milne's headquarters. In March, 1920 he left on indefinite leave.

Thus the situation for a time was that General Franchet d'Espérey commanded the Army of the Danube (General Berthelet) and all troops in the Balkans, including those of Turkey in Europe; General Milne commanded the Allied Forces in Turkey in Europe and those operating in Asia Minor, and, under him, Lieut.-General Maitland Wilson commanded the Allied Troops in Turkey in Europe, that is Thrace, (including the Dardanelles and Bosphorus garrisons). The British Admiral was in undivided command of the Allied Naval forces, and he was also the British High Commissioner with French and Italian coadjutors.

Vice-Admiral Gough-Calthorpe, at the suggestion of the Foreign Office, took over the British Embassy building; he was provided with a diplomatic staff and naval and military attachés, and directed to form Financial and Juridical Commissions. On the 24th November, 1918 General Milne was informed that the High Commissioner was the sole channel of communication with the Turkish Government, and in charge of British interests, to whom also all questions affecting the execution of the Armistice terms should be referred.[1] The French and Italian representatives, having lost military command in Constantinople, gladly co-operated in increasing the power of the High Commissioners.

Lieut.-General Bridges, the liaison officer, having aggravated the relations between the international commanders instead of soothing them, left Constantinople to visit the Balkan countries, Hungary, Poland, Crimea and Caucasus, and, after acting as liaison officer with the principal Greek Army at Smyrna, was recalled on the 10th October, 1920, and his Mission abolished.[2]

The Supreme War Council, sitting at Versailles, throughout supported the contention, put forward in the first case by the British, that they, having beaten the Turks, were entitled to settle matter at Constantinople.

---

[1] In the Rhineland the High Commission did not assume power until the Peace Terms were ratified, and the Inter-Allied Armistice Commission was the channel of communication with the German Government.
[2] See his book, *Alarums and Excursions*.

EFFECTIVE OCCUPATION OF CONSTANTINOPLE: INTER-ALLIED POLICE COMMISSION

On the 11th January, 1919 General Milne was instructed from London to assume executive control of the Constantinople police, thus inaugurating an effective occupation. Under his direction, Lieut.-General Maitland Wilson formed an International Police Commission. On the other hand, the French claimed control of the Turkish Gendarmerie, on the grounds that the commander of the Macedonian gendarmerie when war broke out in 1914 was the French Colonel Goulon, and he arrived to resume his duties.

The police organization gave no trouble. The Commission had British, French and Italian officers as members under a British President, Br.-General F.G. Fuller, Lieut.-General Maitland Wilson's chief General Staff officer,[1] and Constantinople was divided into three zones, Pera and Galata (British), Stambul (French) and Scutari (Italian), one for each nationality. In February these were sub-divided to form six zones, each with two Allied officers and from 35 to 65 Allied police.[2] Military guards were placed on the Embassy, officers' quarters, offices, hospital, banks, prisons and piers, and visual signalling between the international units was arranged. Outside the city attempts to interfere with the railway were dealt with by patrols, and fomenters of disorder were arrested.

Crimes against the property and security of the Allied forces were dealt with by police courts, the more serious cases by military courts appointed for the purpose.[3] Ordinary offences and civil cases were left, as in normal times, to the consular courts under the capitulations, and, if these were non-existent, to the Turkish courts. In addition, an Inter-Allied Sanitary Administration was set up, and, in August, 1919, a Prison Commission for the purpose of the inspection and improvement of prison condition. Under the Allied naval commanders-in-chief, Inter-Allied Captains of the Port were appointed.

In a very short time branches of the Expeditionary Force Canteen and of the Y.M.C.A., an officers' club and a rest house, were established, and the British Seamen's Hospital taken over by the staff of No. 82 General Hospital.

For some time after the occupation no consular courts functioned, and in many cases there were unnecessary delays in Turkish Courts. Eventually the British, French and Italian Governments agreed, in September, 1919, to the establishment of a temporary Inter-Allied Court to deal with Inter-Allied subjects charged with civil offences and civil cases between British, French and Italian subjects on the one hand and the Turkish on the other.

The High Commissioners decided that the following might be taken to enjoy the privileges of the capitulations: British, French, Italian, Greek, Rumanians proper, Poles formerly Russian subjects, Poles who were formerly German subjects only after peace with Germany had been ratified, and certain others after peace with Austria had been ratified. These decisions were notified to General Milne, as General Officer Commanding the Army of the Black Sea, by the British High Commissioner, now Admiral Sir John de Robeck: at the same time he pointed out that an Inter-Allied Military Court to try criminal offences also seemed desirable, as

---

[1] In February, 1920 he was relieved by Colonel C.R. Ballard, the combined police and General Staff work having grown too onerous for one officer.
[2] The establishment of the Turkish Police was only 2,064, and it was about 500 short.
[3] Summary police courts under any duly appointed officer: one month and £50; second police courts, under a field officer: 2 months and £100; military courts: 6 months and £400. For grave offences G.H.Q. assembled a court.

Hellenic subjects were especially troublesome, and the Turkish courts could not punish them, even detain them in prison, as Greece was our Ally, and there was no Greek court to try them. There was also the question of offences committed, say, by British subjects in the French zone, Stambul.

General Milne in reply, pointed out that such an Inter-Allied Court had no organization to execute its judgments, no prison in which its sentences might be carried out, and that, during the Armistice, the senior military officer, in this case, General Franchét d'Espérey, would seem to be the controlling and reviewing authority.

The Supreme Council at Versailles was busily engaged on the Peace Treaty with Germany and, in any case, was not troubling about Turkey, as it was assumed that the U.S.A. would, under the authority of the League of Nations, accept a mandate to govern Turkey, or, at least, to protect Armenia. So nothing about the complicated questions of the various jurisdictions had been settled by October, 1920, when General Milne was relieved by General Sir Charles Harington; but, under the authority of the High Commissioner, who had no *locus standi* during the Armistice, a court was created.

EXECUTION OF THE ARMISTICE TERMS

No records of an Inter-Allied Armistice Commission can be found, but the High Commissioners instituted an Inter-Allied Commission "to deal with questions that arise under the Armistice". A chiefs Of Staff Committee consisting of the chief of staff of the British, French and Italian contingents, who took it in turns to be chairman, met once a week, and dealt with outstanding questions. An Inter-Allied Commission was established to deal with administrative questions, including requisitioning in Constantinople areas; a Prisoners of War Reception Committee was formed, as all Allied prisoners were brought to Constantinople. The guns on the Asiatic side of the Dardanelles were destroyed by parties of the Navy. Two wireless stations in the Gallipoli Peninsula were taken over by the Navy, and the others by a joint British and French staff. A joint organization, by Lieut.-General Maitland Wilson's order, took control of the 12 German and Austro-Hungarian banks. The sub-division of Asia Minor into three spheres of influence was at once observed, as put in the Tripartite Agreement signed by the representatives of Great Britain, France and Italy at the same time as the unratified Treaty of Sèvres of the 10th August, 1920.

Under Article 15 of the Armistice terms, the railways of the Ottoman Empire were placed under Allied control. Early in January, 1919 it was decided by the Supreme Council that executive control of the lines in Asia Minor should be chiefly in British hands, and those in Turkey in Europe in French hands. A Commission, composed of the French and British Directors of Railways and their assistants, for the purpose of co-ordinating and regulating the methods of control in both spheres of influence was formed.

The railways involved were:
 The Oriental Railway (in Europe);
 The Ottoman Anatolian Railway;
 The Smyrna-Cassaba & Extension Railway;
 The Ottoman Aidin Railway (Smyrna);
 The Mudania-Brusa Railway (only 20 miles long).

The first two lines were enemy-owned, and staffed in the higher ranks by enemy subjects

(Germans, Austrians, etc.). The remaining three were Allied owned railways, but their directorates had been turned out by the Turks during the War.

On the 13th January, 1919 Br.-General G.B. Rhodes, the British Director of Railways, with a military staff, took control of the Anatolian Railway (Haidar Pasha to Konia, a length of 300 miles, with a branch line from Eskishehr to Ankara, a length of about 200 miles). The Baghdad Railway, which joins the Anatolian line at Konia, remained under the control of General Allenby's Palestine force. Br.-General Rhodes also took control of the Smyrna- Aidin line. To afford protection to the railway staff, British detachments were placed at the main stations, and they occupied Ankara, Konia, Afium Kara Hissar, Eskishehr, Ismid (at the base of the Ismid Peninsula, 50 miles from Constantinople).

Soon after the taking over of the railways, the Supreme Council decided to send an Italian battalion to Konia, which was in the Italian sphere of influence, and it eventually took over the guarding of the Anatolian Railway between Konia and Afium Kara Hissar. Owing to lack of troops, the British detachments at Brusa, Mudania and Ankara had very soon to be withdrawn.

Arrangements were made to house the troops in the most comfortable and healthiest manner in barracks and houses during summer, with very few in the forts; part of the Medical School at Haidar Pasha, for instance, was occupied by a battalion;- and the granting of leave was continued, a party of 2 officers and fifty other ranks proceeding to the United Kingdom nearly every week.

TURKISH DEMOBILIZATION AND HANDING OVER OF ARMS

As far as can be made out, the Constantinople Government were perfectly willing to demobilize the Army and reduce their force to 50,000 and to hand over equipment, etc., and began to do so under supervision of Allied Control Officers. No opposition to demobilization and disarmament was offered except in the Erzeroum area and in the eastern vilayets, where some resistance to surrender of arms; but even there the main difficulty was snowing up of communications with the approach of winter.

On the 21st November, 1919 the Turkish Government reported to General Milne that the 18 oldest classes (1866-83) had been demobilized, and 11 more would have gone by the 1st December, leaving 4, just enough for the purposes of maintaining order. According to an Intelligence report on the Nationalist Movement, until the landing of the Greeks in Smyrna in May, 1919, the Government in Constantinople had sufficient authority in the provinces to ensure the carrying into effect of the terms of the Armistice. Up to May the steady flow into Constantinople of the surrendered armaments from the provinces, including material captured from the British, was a sure indication that the leaders had no thought of further resistance; even at Erzeroum the number of effectives and the armament of the corps under General Kiazim Karabekir were reduced, but not to the figures fixed; in the month of May General Mustapha Kemal (by October the leader of the whole movement) sent in a large consignment of machine guns.

The arms, collected at named centres for each division, were stored in the forts under British charge; but the French objecting to this, one fort on the Dardanelles was handed over to them.[1] Ammunition was also stored, but later dumped into the sea. The checking of the arms, etc., was carried out under British officers.

---

[1] This fort was seized, and the arms removed by Nationalists agents ferried across from Asia, as will be seen.

THE NATIONALIST MOVEMENT

RISE OF THE NATIONALIST MOVEMENT[1]

The occupation of South-West Asia Minor by Italian detachments, and the landing of the Greeks in Smyrna on the 15th May in order to take possession of the Smyrna Zone, as authorized by the Supreme Council, changed the situation in regard to the delivery of arms and ammunition. The surrender of armament from Central and Eastern Anatolia entirely ceased, and during June the formation of two native organizations were reported, one sponsored by the Minister of War, and the other by the former Minister of Marine. Under the first, which divided Asia Minor into two inspectorates, normally to ensure peace, Kemal Pasha was appointed G.O.C. of the northern, and "Little" Djemal Pasha of the Southern inspectorate. These officers used their powers to rouse the people. The agitation became so serious that Kemal was summoned to Constantinople; but he refused to come. He was accordingly dismissed from the Army. Shortly afterwards, he summoned a Congress of the six eastern vilayets at Erzeroum, which on the 7th August, 1919, in fear that Turkish territory would be handed over to the Greeks and the Armenians, issued a proclamation declaring its purpose "to put into action the forces of the nation; to impose the will of the nation in order to maintain the integrity of the Ottoman motherland and the independence of our nation; and to preserve the Caliphate.... We hope that the Entente will abandon the idea of dividing our country". As a first step, the Congress proposed the dismissal of the Grand Vizier and his Cabinet, as they had done nothing to defend the national rights at Smyrna, and Kemal declared, "Henceforth Stambul does not control Anatolia; but Anatolia, Stambul".

A second conference was held at Sivas, which differed from that at Erzeroum in that its delegates came from the whole of Turkey. It decided to seize the telegraph offices all over the country, thus cutting off the Constantinople Government from its supporters in the Provinces, and small parties of soldiers took possession of the offices without difficulty; for the Army in the Provinces, though a mere cadre, was wholly on the Nationalist side. The messages of the British officers were not, however, interfered with. The Constantinople Government, in the last week of September, offered to despatch a few thousand troops; which they believed would restore the situation, as the bodies of Nationalist troops moving about were small and mere escorts to agitators. This offer was declined and, as if to avoid any commitment, on the 15th August the withdrawal of British troops from Transcaucasia was begun, and, on the 7th September, 27th Division headquarters was opened at Batum; on the 14th and 15th, the 81st and 82nd Brigades were disbanded and, on the 24th, the division, the G.O.C. handing over to the Military Governor of Batum, Br.-General J.N. Cooke-Collis, commanding the 80th Brigade.[2] On the 4th March, 1920 this officer was appointed to command the Inter-allied Force of Batum, and the force was withdrawn by the 14th July, 1920. Attempts were made to interfere with the railways, both in Thrace and Anatolia; so, on the 19th September, 1919, a mixed force under Br,-General R.E. Solly-Flood was sent to Eskishehr to support the posts between Ismid and Afium Kara Hissar.

On the 20th October, 1919, General Milne, in reporting on the Nationalist Movement, warned the War Office:

"If the decisions of the Peace Conference are so drastic in the treatment of Turkey

---

[1] An account of the Nationalist revolt, translated from Turkish, will be found in the *Army Quarterly*, April and July, 1926.
[2] Men whose time had not expired were transferred to the 28th Division.

that the older men who have the spirit of compromise are unable to keep the wilder in check, then it will turn out that the Nationalist Movement has very greatly prejudiced the military position of the Allies. The population is armed and now united for the first time; and it is difficult to calculate the force which might be available in the event of a nation rising".

The first order directing preparations to be made to meet possible enterprises of the Nationalist Movement forces and bands in their pay was issued, and directions were given for the first reconnaissances to be made of lines to defend Constantinople from the east and west. The essential parts of the armament of the Bosphorus and Dardanelles defences were removed to storage at Constantinople.

A week later, that he and not a British commander might control the situation, General Franchet d'Espérey, removed the French 122nd Division from the Allied corps, declared it to be the general reserve of the Allied Army of the Orient, and replaced it by six battalions under General Cot, four Senegalese and two French (one of which was reserved for the French G.H.Q. guard).

An agreement was made in October between Turkey and Soviet Russia, with a view to co-operation in the Caucasus and to trading; and this, no doubt, helped to stiffen the Nationalist attitude. Kemal required time to organize, and this the Allies gave him. In the same month a general election was held throughout Turkey, which the Nationalist won by a substantial majority; the cabinet resigned and the new Grand Vizier opened negotiations with Kemal. The Nationalist deputies of the new assembly met at Ankara, drew up a declaration of their arms, and rejected any division of Anatolia.

That military precaution were necessary was soon made evident; for, on the 28th January, 1920, a Nationalist band raided the fort of Akbash, on the European side of the Dardanelles, guarded only by seven Senegalese; and carried off to Panderma, on the southern side of the Sea of Marmora, 30 machine guns, 8,500 rifles and 500,000 rounds of small arms ammunition, where they were taken over by a Nationalist detachment. Lieut.-General Maitland Wilson thereupon sent a hundred Punjabis to Gallipoli to remove all the Turkish machine-gun plates and the rifle bolts of the arms still in the forts, and to dump the ammunition into the sea; and he gave orders that French troops in the Dardanelles were not to be used for guarding depots of arms. The Turks placed every obstacle in the way of enquiry at Panderma, and at Derindje (a small naval base, 5 miles west of Ismid) the local authorities tried to oppose the shipment of arms to Malta.

Breaches of the Armistice becoming of almost daily occurrence, and obstruction and bad faith being evident, the High Commissioner, by ultimatum, demanded the removal from office of Djemal Pasha, the Minister of War, and of Djevad Pasha, the chief of the General Staff. Intimation that they had resigned was received within the time limit of 48 hours. The secret hostilities activities of the Minister of War, however, in collusion with the Nationalist, and the certain transfer of arms, were continued under their successors. The effective military occupation of Constantinople was the only remedy.

FORMAL OCCUPATION OF CONSTANTINOPLE

The next events of importance, therefore, are that, in February 1920, the Supreme Council decided that the Turkish Government should remain in Constantinople and that, on the 12th March 1920, General Milne was ordered to occupy Constantinople. This he did on the 16th without opposition, using British and Allied troops and strong parties of the Royal and Allied Navies, thus at last making the occupation recognized and formal. The Ministry of War, Admiralty and other offices were occupied, the Ministry of War by an Allied Commission of Control under Br.-General D.I. Shuttleworth (83rd Brigade), with a French and an Italian representative. The actual supervision of the various departments, General Staff, Intendance, Organization, Control, Recruiting, and Inspection of Arms and Ammunition was carried out by pairs of British officers, all under Major O.H. van Millingen. The gendarmerie was disarmed, and hostile Ministers were arrested and deported to Malta. The post, telegraphs and telephones were taken under control of an Inter-Allied Committee, with Lieut.-Colonel C.E.T. Rolland as president. Lieut.-General Maitland Wilson, as Allied commander in Constantinople, issued a proclamation warning the inhabitants to "refrain from all acts in any way inimical to "the Allied forces".

In view of the feeling which the occupation of Constantinople was sure to arouse and the increasingly hostile attitude of the Nationalist Movement, General Milne decided to close the Anatolian Railway east of Ismid and withdraw all Allied troops. The Italians at first demurred, but after a little delay consented.

In February 1920, after the railway bridge near Eskishehr had been damaged, a special force under Br.-General F.S. Montague-Bates was sent out to hold the ground near whilst it was repaired, so that the posts east of it could be brought in. Their withdrawal was opposed by Nationalist forces, and bridges on either side of Eskishehr were destroyed; but under the protection of Br.-General Montague-Bates's force, by the 27th March all parties had been brought into Ismid, and practically all the rolling stock.

From the 16th March, the War Office decided that the area occupied by the Army of the Black Sea was not an area of active operations, in spite of the protest from General Milne that an army engaged in active operations, entailing on the Asiatic side, constant outpost work and long marches, with four definite engagements, including beating off a five day attack against Ismid, could not be run under peace regulations. This state of affairs, however, continued to obtain until the 28th July.

For service on the Asiatic side, the 242nd Brigade was formed on the 30th March under Br.-General Montague-Bates. It consisted of 1 British battalion, 3 Indian battalions, with the 20th Hussar, artillery, engineers, pioneers, etc., attached, and was stationed around Ismid, covering Scutari and Haidar Pasha. Its orders were to be neutral towards the Nationalists, but not to allow them to penetrate to the west. In order to prevent clashes, the Turkish Government in Constantinople offered and was allowed to send some of its forces east of Ismid. These, when fired on by the Nationalists, fled back to the British wire and, after reference to G.H.Q. were allowed through.

Considering that the presence of Turkish troops in Constantinople constituted a source of weakness to the defence, General Milne decided to disarm and disband them. He issued orders to this effect on the 10th June and after some delay this was carried out.

Trouble had soon begun as to the presidency and membership of the various commissions and committees formed to control the Turkish offices of state, in which at first the French and

Italians seemed to be in no hurry to take part. Armistice conditions still prevailed; that is to say hostilities were not at an end. General Milne was Allied Commander-in-Chief at Constantinople, and of the forces in Asia Minor. In reply to a letter from the British High Commissioner, he pointed out that he had received orders from H.M. Government to carry out the military occupation of Constantinople and to assume control of the Ministry of War, that this was purely a military question, and as long as the representatives of the Allies did not recognize his authority he was unable to discuss the subject. As the French and Italians hesitated in co-operating, he carried on with British officers alone on the new commissions and committees, until Allied commanders accepted his rulings.

The British High Commission was forced to admit that movements and operations of French troops had taken place in Cilicia and an armistice concluded with Mustapha Kemal, who was in open rebellion against the Turkish Government and in direct conflict with the Allies, without any of the facts being conveyed to him by his French colleague.[1] Similarly no communication had been made to him by his Italian colleague in regard to the disembarkation and movement of Italian troops in the South-West portion of Asia Minor. These rifts in the Alliance did not remain unknown to the Turks.

The High Commission apparently ceased to function as regards military affairs; for, on the 16th March, it decided not to issue instructions to the military authorities, but only record decisions based on the instructions of the Supreme Council, leaving each High Commissioner to make any communications to his own military authorities.

To strengthen the position of General Milne, as already mentioned, General Franchet d'Espérey was given indefinite leave; and returned to France. This remained the position until General Sir Charles Harington arrived in October, 1920 to succeed General Milne. The attitude of the Nationalists made it certain that, if given time to organize, they would resist any attempt to break up the Ottoman Empire. In Fact, before the Peace Treaty was signed they had begun to be troublesome. On the 14th June they attacked the Ismid lines, but without success: seamen from *H.M.S. Ramillies*, and the 1/Gordon Highlanders, newly arrived, were ordered up as reinforcements; and all formed Nationalist troops then withdrew.

In order to deal with the expected rising, the Hellenic Government were given authority to cross the Neutral Zone of the Smyrna zone established by General Milne, as Allied Commander-in-Chief in Asia Minor, when he visited the area after the occupation, and to proceed against the Nationalists; and their troops entered Brusa on the 8th July, and they also marched onto Thrace reaching Adrianople on the 25th.

Sniping at Allied troops became frequent, and bands were again reported near the Ismid lines. On the 12th July Major-General Sir Edmund Ironside was placed in command of a force consisting of the 242nd Brigade, the 16th Greek Infantry Regiment, the 29th Hussars (arrived from Egypt on the 4th), two batteries R.F.A., and the 26th Field Company R.E. to clear the Nationalist bands away from the Ismid Peninsula and open communications with the Greek forces to the south. This he accomplished by sending out four small columns.

On the 12th July, too, "Q" Force R.A.F., consisting of headquarters No. 55 Squadron (D.H. 9's and 9A's) and aircraft park arrived at Haidar Pasha, and took over an airfield at Maltepe, three stations down the Anatolian railway.

---

[1] During the winter of 1919-20 Nationalist bands had made attacks in Cilicia, and in April, 1920 forces under Kemal inflicted a defeat on the French. Realizing that a large army would be required to hold Cilicia the French renounced their claims in South-East Asia Minor, and decided to concentrate on establishing their rule in Syria.

ALLIES' REORGANISATION

On the 16th July, 1920 Lieut.-General Maitland Wilson issued the following proclamation:

"Owing to the presence of Turkish armed forces, hostile to the allies, in the area west of the Bosphorus, and to the presence of armed bands of brigands who take this opportunity to attack the peaceful inhabitants of the county, it is notified that henceforward:
1. Any person found in possession of firearms or bombs, or with firearms or bombs in his house, will be tried by an Allied Military Court, and will on conviction be condemned to death or such other penalty as may be decided by the court.
2. The owner, or occupier, of any house from which fire is directed upon Allied troops will be required to identify the individual, or individuals, guilty of firing, or, in default, will be tried by an Allied Military Court for giving assistance to the enemies of the Allied Forces."

It was conjected that the attacks on the Ismid line were organized with the purpose of obtaining possession of a large depôt of ammunitions at Derindje. All small arms ammunition had already been removed, and now, by General Milne's order, the depôt was evacuated, and all Turkish munitions stored there were destroyed. As danger seemed to threaten the railway from Ismid to Constantinople, he decided to rely in future on communications by sea.

During the later part of July and during August the villages on the Asiatic side of the Bosphorus, Sea of Marmora and the Dardanelles were searched for arms, and during September small Allied columns were on the move, and had occasional affrays with Nationalist bands. On the 20th August, on Major-General Ironside's departure for North Persia, his force was broken up, and the 242nd Brigade came under the 28th Division. On the 17th September the Greek Mannissa Division, under General Gargalides, began arriving by sea at Derindje, and on the 25th he took over the Ismid front. In consequence of this, on the 28th a redistribution was made of the Allied Corps for the defence of Constantinople and the maintenance of order:

Section I. Pera and Galata:

G.O.C. 85th Brigade:
 1 British battalion, 2 Indian, 1 French, 1 Senegalese, 1 Italian, Greek detachment;
 1 British battery, and 1 field company; a landing party of marines.

Section II. Stambul:

G.O.C. French Contingent:
 (1) Base Militaire: 2 Senegalese; 1 section of Armoured Cars; and 1 landing party.
 (2) 85th Brigade Group: ½ British battalion, 2 Indian.

Section III. Scutari and Kadikeui (South of Scutari):

G.O.C. 28th Division:
 1 British battalion, 2 Indian

ALLIES' REORGANISATION

General Reserve:

½ British battalion; 1 battery.
In addition to the above a distribution map shows:
at Therapia, ½ Indian battalion; at Kuchuk Chekmedje training ground, 1 Indian battalion; at Mashlak (training ground north of Constantinople), 1 British battalion.

Along the Asiatic shore of the Sea of Marmora between Scutari and the Gulf of Ismid:

at Haidar Pasha, 1 British battalion and armoured train; at Bostandjik, 1 British battalion, 1 Indian and 1 field company; at Pavlo, 20th Hussars, 1 British battalion, ½ Indian Pioneer battalion (rest distributed); and close by, at Tuzla, 1 British battalion, 1 howitzer battery; and an Indian battalion divided between Sileh and Chanak (but the last named placed was in September reinforced by the sending the 2/East Surrey there).

The total French force, all on the European side, in October was 1 French infantry regiment, 2 battalions of African Tirailleurs and 4 of Senegalese; one squadron Moroccan Spahis, a group of field artillery, an armoured car company, one air squadron, and services.

THE UNRATIFIED PEACE TREATY OF SÊVRES

The terms of a Treaty of Peace were handed to the Turkish delegation on the 11th May 1920 and, after three months of procrastination, the treaty was signed at Sèvres on the 10th August 1920, that is nearly a year and ten months after the Armistice, and then only under duress. On the 17th July, signature being withheld, the Turks were given ten days, to midnight 27th/28th July to sign.[1] The treaty was drawn on the lines of the Peace Treaty with Germany (ratified on the 19th January 1920), and was very lengthy, containing 425 Articles. It not only deprived Turkey of Syria, Mesopotamia, Palestine, Armenia (boundaries to be fixed by Commission) and the Hedjaz, and of any claim to suzerainty of Egypt and Cyprus, but also (Articles 57-61) created an International Commission to control, practically to rule, over the "Zone of the Straits" – shown on a map as including territory on both shores of the Dardanelles, of the Sea of Marmora, and of the Bosphorus, with the islands Samothrace, Imbros, Lemnos and Mytilene at the western end. It also transferred (Articles 65-63) to the Greeks the Turkish rights of sovereignty over Smyrna and an area of territory around that city. It was to the cession of the Smyrna enclave and to the international control of the straits that the Nationalists objected.

The Army of Occupation was affected by the provision (Articles 196-205) for "Inter-Allied Commissions and Control and Organization".[2]

The extent to which Turkey was to be disarmed and what forces she might keep were laid down (Articles 152-207). The navy was reduced to a few sloops and torpedo boats for police and fishing duties, and no submarines and no air forces were permitted.

The armed forces, to be recruited for 12 years' service by voluntary enlistment only – officers were to serve 25 years – were limited to (1) the Sultan's bodyguard of 700 men (its composition was given in detail); (2) troops o f gendarmerie, not to exceed 35,000 to maintain order; and (3) "special elements", not to exceed 15,000, intended to reinforce the gendarmerie in the case of serious trouble, and eventually to secure control of the frontiers. The authorized maximum of armaments and munitions supplies was given in details; no tanks, no armoured cars, no gas, and no flame-throwers were permitted.

The number of military schools was fixed and it was stated that other educational establishments, clubs and societies might not occupy themselves with military matters. Customs officials, police, Forest Guards were limited to the 1913 establishment, with proportional increase according to any increase in the local population. The fortifications of the Straits were to be demolished, other fortifications disarmed. War Criminals were to be handed over for trial.

It was to be the business of the Inter-Allied Commission of Control and Organization to supervise the execution of military, naval and air clauses, and represent the principal Allied Powers in all matters relating to all matters of the execution.

For the Financial Clauses a Financial Commission was to be appointed; it virtually displaced the Turkish Treasury, as all the resources of Turkey, except those allocated to the service of the Ottoman National Debt were placed at its disposal. The chairmanship was to be held by the French, British and Italian Delegates in turn.

For control of the "Zone of the Straits" a "Commission of the Straits" was to be formed, composed of representatives of the U.S.A. (if willing), British Empire, France, Italy, Japan and Russia, each with two votes, and representatives of Greece, Rumania, Bulgaria, and Turkey, each with one vote. It was practically an independent harbour board, with its own flag, own budget

---

[1] For the principal Articles see Appendix IV.
[2] These Articles are given in full in Appendix II.

and separate organization. In case of interference with the freedom of navigation, it might, through the representatives at Constantinople of the Allied Powers, call for naval and military aid.

The territorial or other security was taken to ensure the execution of the terms of the Treaty, and no mention was made of a period of occupation – it had been 15 years in the case of the Rhineland.

THE TRIPARTITE AGREEMENT

On the same date as the Treaty of Sèvres was signed a "Tripartite Agreement" was come to between the British Empire, France and Italy respecting their spheres of influence and other matters in Anatolia.[1] Excluding Smyrna and the Zone of the Straits, to France was allotted the south-east, to Italy the south-west, leaving the northern belt to the Turks; but the agreement was not to come into force until the Treaty of Peace was ratified.

THE STRENGTH OF THE ALLIED ARMY OF OCCUPATION

On the date of the signature of the Peace Treaty, the 10th August 1920, the Allied Corps of Occupation consisted of the British 28th Division, with the 242nd Brigade attached, with a total of a British cavalry regiment, 8 battalions, 11 Indian battalions, and the divisional troops, distributed as mentioned above, with one squadron R.A.F.; a French contingent of 3 French and 6 native battalions; an Italian contingent of 2 battalions; a Greek contingent of 1 battalion and 1 Cretan regiment, with a Greek division about to take over the Ismid front. The Turkish garrison of Constantinople, under the local, and more or less puppet, Government there, was 2,993 infantry and 195 cavalry, with 983 foot and 24 mounted gendarmes. Clearing operations in Eastern Thrace had nearly been concluded by Hellenic forces, one division of which was being transferred to Smyrna. In the Smyrna area the Greeks had a large Army of about 90,000 men, which it was proposed to reduce to 50,000 men. Under the authority of the Supreme Council, given in view of the weakness of the Allies in and around Constantinople and the Straits, and of the fact that the Greeks alone had sufficient forces on the spot to stave off the danger of the Nationalists approaching the areas, the Greeks had advanced beyond the line, fixed by General Milne, known as "The Balfour Line", which limited their enclave; and were operating in the third phase of their plan, in which they hoped to reach Afion Kara Hissar (on the Anatolian railway 70 miles south of Eskishehr) – Eskishehr. A fatal area it was to prove for Hellenic arms. Ready to oppose them was a force of Turks, estimated at 18,000 but soon to rising to 50,000, with some German aeroplanes, and aided by a number of bands, some of them over a thousand strong. Columns from Ismid were dealing with "brigands", who, among other things, had several times damaged the railway bridges near Eskishehr.

A treaty is only effective as long as it can be enforced. One after another, the treaties made at the termination of wars have been thrown over by the Powers temporarily bound by them, as soon as they felt strong enough to do so. The strength of the Nationalist Movement in Turkey was overlooked, and it was assumed that the Ottoman Empire, the "sick man" of Europe for so many years, was at last moribund and would give no further trouble.

---

[1] Appendix III.

ORDERS FOR THE REDUCTION OF THE BRITISH CONTINGENT

The international garrison at Batum had been withdrawn in July. On the 13th August the War Office ordered the reduction of the Army of the Black Sea by two British battalions, which were to return at once, and by two Indian battalions to be followed by others, without relief.[1] It was proposed to transfer the British cavalry regiment to Egypt and "Q" Air Force (less a few old machines to be sold to the Greeks) to Mesopotamia, where it was badly wanted (it left on the 3rd September). The intention was that the force should gradually reduced to four British and four Indian battalions for the garrison of the "Zone of the Straits".

On the 29th September 1920 a telegram was received by G.H.Q. from the War Office announcing that the "Army of the Black Sea will be reduced to two infantry brigades, each consisting of one British and two Indian Battalions, one field artillery brigade and one company of Royal Engineers, as soon as the situation permits", and General Milne was asked to suggest the auxiliary units required and the composition of the headquarters of this force.

THE NEW ORGANIZATION OF THE INTERNATIONAL FORCE

The telegram continued that over and above this force, there would be at Constantinople a British corps headquarters under a lieutenant-general, who would have under his command the above British force, the French force, also approximating to a weak division, and possibly an Italian force and a Greek division; this Allied force would be responsible solely for the security of the Straits, and would be concentrated in all probability in the vicinity of Constantinople and the Dardanelles: active operations in the interior of Asia Minor were not to be undertaken by it.

The telegram added as regards the Peace Terms that information would be sent later of the organization of the various commissions which were to be formed, and that the British commander of the Allied forces would probably be appointed President of these commissions.

GENERAL HARINGTON ARRIVES TO TAKE COMMAND

At the end of October General Sir Charles Harington arrived at Constantinople to be commander of the Allied forces. The acceptance of a British general as Commander-in-Chief by the French was due to the personal intervention of Maréchal Foch.[2] His instructions from the Chief of the Imperial General Staff were to make friends with the Allies, to lay a good foundation for the gendarmerie and to keep clear of politics. On the 1st November Sir Horace Rumbold, Bart., a professional diplomat, became Ambassador at Constantinople,[3] but he signed letters to the commander of the Allied forces and to the Commission of Control and

---

[1] A relief was in progress. During September one Indian battalion had left and was followed in October by 5 others. Two were arriving at the end of October.

[2] The date of arrival is not given in the war diaries. General Harington's book, "Tim Harington Looks Back", says that he arrived "at the end of October". He signed the General Staff war diary for October.

[3] Foreign Office List 1921.

Organization as "High Commissioner". On the 8th November Major-General (later Sir) Thomas Marden, who had arrived a week earlier, took over command of the reduced British force.[1]

The headquarters of the Inter-Allied Corps, under Lieut.-General Maitland Wilson, were broken up and their archives taken over by G.H.Q.[2]

CHANGE IN THE SITUATION
KING CONSTANTINE RETURNS

Beyond the probability of disorders in Constantinople and Scutari, for the suppression of which schemes had been prepared, there was no apprehension of much military trouble; for the Turkish armed forces were not judged to be formidable, and the Greeks were organized and in considerable force in Asia Minor, as well as in Europe. In little over one month, however, this situation was materially affected by two events: first, the defeat of the southern White Russians, under General Wrangel, based on the Crimea, with the consequent influx in to Constantinople of 120,000 Russian refugees, 30,000 of them soldiers with arms and ammunition. The armed men were dispersed into camps at Gallipoli and elsewhere under French supervision; but as this irked them, due precautions had to be taken to prevent them marching on Constantinople.

The second event, also in December 1920, the defeat at the Greek elections of the Prime Minister, Venizelos, and the return to Athens of King Constantine, was more serious. As Constantine was not recognized by the Allies, the Hellenic troops ceased to be under the Allied Commander-in-Chief, and as the King replaced war experienced Venizelist officers by untried Royalists, the value of the Greek troops was seriously diminished.

The reaction of these two events on the Army of Occupation will be dealt with later.

ALLIED DIFFERENCES OVER COMMAND

The more immediate troubles were diplomatic, in connection with the immediate acceptance of General Harington as Allied Commander-in-Chief, and as to the presidency and membership of the various commissions. In China, in the Boxer expedition of 1900, the difficulty of a united command had been got over by the Kaiser declaring the Field-Marshal Graf Waldersee to be "international" and removing his name from the Prussian Army List.[3] The Italians were ready to accept a British General at once; but it was not until June 1921 that the French agreed to his immediate assumption of power, after arguing that his two years' tenure of office – when he would be succeeded by a Frenchman and Italian in turn – should not begin until the ratification of the Peace Treaty. General Charpy, in command of the French contingent, throughout affected to act independently of the united command.

It had been agreed in Versailles that the General Officer Commanding the Allied Forces and

---

[1] At the War Office, before leaving London, General Sir Henry Wilson, the G.I.C.S., said to him, "You are going to the quietest part of the British Empire". (Army Quarterly, xxvi, p. 265).
[2] The strengths of G.H.Q. Staffs under Generals Milne and Harington are given in Appendix VI.
[3] Waldersee was readily obeyed by all the contingents except the German, which declined to accept orders except from a German.

the President of the Inter-Allied Military Commission of Control should be one of the same person.[1] The "general duties" of the British Commander-in-Chief were then defined as:

A. Command
1. Disposition of:
    i   British forces of occupation,
    ii French forces of occupation,
    iii Italian forces of occupation,
    iv Greek divisions on Ismid Peninsula and any Greek troops in the Special Zone around Constantinople,
    v   Such Turkish and Greek gendarmerie as might be employed in the Special Zone around Constantinople.

2. Liaison with the main Greek Army.

B. Supervision
Supervision of the sub-commissions of control and organization.

The relationship of the Commander-in-Chief to the High Commissioners remained unsettled, and a case in point arose in June 1921, when General Harington had 60 Russian Bolshevists arrested and deported. The French and Italian High Commissioners held that, as expulsion was a political matter, they should have been consulted, and that the Allied Commander-in-Chief should confine himself to military affairs. General Harington, naturally, pointed out that as the Peace Treaty had not been ratified a technical state of war still existed, and that he was responsible for the safety of the Army. The British Government took the view that General Harington was in no way responsible to the High Commissioners – who, for convenience, were engaged on normal diplomatic work as ambassadors – but that he should keep in close touch with them, and be available in a consultative capacity; that he was free to act in matter affecting the safety of the Allied troops, in the maintenance of order, and in the administration of the laws and regulations of occupied territory; and that he was responsible to the Allied Army Council for British affairs, and the senior French and Italian commanders for their affairs. It was, however, settled on the 15th August that the French and Italian generals should be consulted about, and kept informed of, any action, but that their approval was not necessary. These solutions were accepted on that date by the French and Italian High Commissioners in reliance on the system pursued by General Harington, although they dissented from the principle that he was not responsible to the High Commissioners, and reserved the right to raise the question should he, in their opinion, exceed his power. International affairs rely greatly on personalities for their successful working, and much depends on the selection of suitable agents. Owing to the tact of General Harington, this compromise worked very well; but it would seem that throughout what followed the British Government favoured the Greeks, and the French Government, aided by the Italian, actively supported the Turks.

The attempt of the High Commissioners to make themselves the de facto Government of Turkey, and the Allied Army their instrument during an armistice may be said to have failed.

---

[1] In Germany and Bulgaria the similar commissions had been presided over by Frenchmen, and in Austria and Hungary by Italians.

THE DIRECTING COMMITTEE

But in July 1921, hostilities on land between the Turks and Greeks being in progress, and the Greek fleet still off Constantinople and using the city as a base for supplies, when General Harington, after fixing a neutral boundary on land, advocated that a neutral line should be drawn on the water, he was overruled by the High Commission.

By an order issued on the 8th September 1921, General Harington cleared up the juridical situation.[1]

THE SUB-COMMISSIONS

The instructions for the constitution and functions of the Inter-Allied Commission of Control and Organization referred to in the Peace Treaty were drawn up by the Allied Military Committee of Versailles and adopted on the 22nd September 1920.[2]

It was originally proposed to make two sub-commissions, one for control, that is for demobilization and disarmament, and the other for organization of the gendarmerie and the Army. In making up the sub-commissions, General Harington, as President of the Inter- Allied Commission of Control and Organization, wished that a British officer, Major-General G. McK. Franks, should be president of the sub-commission of organization, and to this the Supreme Council agreed (13th September 1920). Objecting to this arrangement was subsequently raised by the French as placing too much power in the hands of the British Commander-in-Chief. The French still claimed supremacy in the matter of the gendarmerie, because a French officer, Colonel Foulon had been head of the pre-war Macedonian gendarmerie, and since the occupation had tried to function again, but had not been recognized, and had then died. He had followed an Italian, so it might be argued that it was the turn of a British officer. It was eventually agreed that there should be three sub-commissions instead of two, "Organization" being divided into "Gendarmerie" and "Special Elements", over which the French and British, respectively, should preside, and that an Italian officer should be president of the Disarmament Sub-Commission, each Power, therefore, having a president.

THE DIRECTING COMMITTEE OF GENERALS

Another move to reduce British influence was a proposal from the French and Italians to form a committee of generals as an intermediary between General Harington and the Sub-commissions. In a letter dated 1st February 1921[3] to the Chief of the Imperial General Staff, the British Commander-in-Chief protested against this as unnecessary, and pointed out that he was asked "to accept a position in which the British representation is altogether too small, and from which no constructive success can be obtained. A French general [Pellé] is coming as Ambassador.

"The President of the Financial Commission is to be French; the President of the Naval Commission is to be French. There will be a French general on the Committee of Generals."

"The President of the Sub-Commission of Organization [subsequently changed to Sub-Commission of Gendarmerie] is to be French."

---

[1] Appendix V.
[2] These lengthy instructions are in War Office file 6152/5548 enclosure 42b.
[3] In file, Committee of Control and Organization, Vol. ii.

THE COMMISSIONS

"The President of the Sub-Commission of Control [subsequently changed to Sub-Commission of Disarmament] is to be Italian."

He also asked for the elimination of the Committee of Generals and dealt with the urgent need of gendarmerie as an essential in the restoration of Turkey (a week later he put forward a complete scheme); and he pressed for the definite recognition of his own position as Inter-Allied Commander-in-Chief and President of the Commission of Control and Organization, and for the appointment of Major-General Franks as President of the Sub-Commission of Organization.

The War Office on 10th February forwarded General Harington's letter to the Foreign Office, saying that the Army Council found itself in complete agreement with his statement of the case. It has been seen how the last two points had been settled; as regards the Committee of Generals, to was allowed to stand, but with General Harington as President and French and Italian commanders as members. General Mombelli, who always got on well with the British, was appointed as Italian member.

The Directing Committee of Generals, as it was called, held regular meetings; its records were kept in English, and its orders to the sub-commissions went forth in the name of the President, signed by the British Secretary, Lieut.-Colonel T.G.G. Heywood, instead of in the name of the Allied Commander-in-Chief.

THE MANY COMMISSIONS

For record, it many be stated that the following other Commissions were set up:
Commission of the Straits
Judicial Commission (British, French, Italian, Japanese);
Financial Commission (British, French, Italian, with Turks attached);
Arbitral Commission (League of Nations);
Kurdistan Commission in Constantinople (British, French, Italian);
Boundary Commission for Zone of the Straits (British, French, Italian);
Boundary Commission for Syria and Mesopotamia (British, French, Italian and Turk);
Boundary Commission for Greece (4 principal Allies, Greek and Turk);
Boundary Commission for Smyrna Territory (British, French, Italian, Greek and Turks);
Boundary Commission for Kurdistan (British, French, Italian, Persian, Kurd);
Boundary Commission for Free Zone of Smyrna (Turks, Greek, League of Nations);
Arbitration Commission for Armenia and its boundaries;
Maritza Commission (League of Nations).

THE SUB-COMMISSIONS

FORMATION OF THE SUB-COMMISSIONS

Although the Treaty of Sèvres had not been ratified, after the above various delays steps were taken in Constantinople to form the various commissions and start work. On the 31st October the Directing Committee of Generals requested the Liaison Section to inform the Ottoman Minister of War that the three sub-commissions had been constituted, and consequently room must be found in the War Office for the two dealing with Disarmament and Special Elements at the earliest possible date. On the 16th November 1921 the Directing Committee of Generals, by letter, requested the High Commissioners to inform the Ottoman Government of the institution of the Military Inter-Allied Commission of Control and Organization and its sub-commissions.

The Sub-Commission of Control of Disarmament was formed, provisionally, on the 13th September, under the Presidency of an Italian, Major-General Bassionano, and it was instructed by the Directing Committee of Generals to constitute a Committee of Enquiry into the Ottoman Government factories. This Sub-Commission continued to function until the final settlement in 1923, arranging for the removal, sale or destruction of the arms of the demobilized divisions which had been delivered.

The Sub-Commission of Gendarmerie was formed on the 20th September 1921, with a French President, Major-General Fillonneau.[1] Arrangements were made for three spheres, following the division of Asia Minor under the Tripartite Agreement, in which British, French and Italian officers supervised the force. A number of recruits were raised, but they gradually slipped away – the officers first – to join Nationalist forces, and the scheme never materialised.

The Sub-Commission of Special Elements was also formed on the 20th September 1921, with Major-General Franks as President. Its instructions from the Directing Committee of Generals were:-

a. to superintend the organization of the Ottoman War Office;
b. to superintend the execution of the military orders given by the Ottoman War Office, with the exception of those concerning Disarmament and Gendarmerie; but, within the precincts of the Ottoman War Office, the actual supervision was to be carried out by the Inter-Allied Liaison Section (see following page), acting as representative of the various sub-commissions;
c. to co-operate with the Sub-Commission of Disarmament and Gendarmerie regarding certain requirements;
d. to study future requirements; and
e. to work out and submit proposal for the organization of the Special Elements.[2] This Sub-Commission was unable to accomplish much. It made studies for the reduction of the Ottoman War Office, and for the evacuation of Anatolia by the Greek forces, and proposals by direction of the Directing Committee of Generals for the accommodation of military orphans.

---

[1] His mother and one grandmother were English, he spoke English as if it were his native tongue, and was more than friendly inclined to the British.
[2] Major-General Sir George Franks reports that he was employed on a number of odd jobs, such as conducting commissions of enquiry into the atrocities the Greeks and Turks perpetrated on each other, carrying out the exchange of British and Turkish prisoners of war, and commanding the British troops when Major-General Marden was otherwise employed.

THE INTER-ALLIED LIAISON SECTION

The Allied Commission of Control of the Ottoman War Office set up when Constantinople was occupied in March 1920, was renamed the "Inter-Allied Liaison Section", in whish the three Powers were represented, Colonel A.T. Bechwith remaining the President. This Section had no executive powers. It duties were:

(1) Liaison, in which capacity it was to transmit to the Ottoman Minister of War all orders and instructions issued by the President of the Directing Committee of Generals, or say any of the sub-commissions.

(2) Supervision, in which capacity it was to supervise the execution of all such orders in the Ottoman War Office.

(3) Information, in which capacity it was to supply all information which it obtained, or asked to obtain, to the Directing Committee and sub-commissions.

The Ottoman Minister of War from first to last recognized the Liaison Section, but he and his colleagues saw no necessary for the formation of the sub-commissions, and accepted them only under protest. The room required in the Ministry of War were handed over, and returns of the strength of the Turkish Army (steadily about 8,000) – not of the Nationalist Army – were rendered at intervals. In general, the Section formed a useful channel.

THE TURKISH-GREEK STRUGGLE

For eighteen months, during 1921 and until July 1922, the Allied troops were the spectators of a struggle between the Nationalist Turk forces, under Kemal, and the Greeks, which was to involve the complete withdrawal of the latter from Asia Minor. Their own operations were limited to putting down brigands in the area near Constantinople, and to occasional infantry raids. In conjunction with the French, a wired line of defence had in 1921 been constructed across the Ismid Peninsula, about fifteen miles east of Scutari, and the Chatalja lines, which cover Constantinople on the west, had been kept in repair by our Allies. In the early months of 1922, all the Indian battalions were withdrawn and replaced by three British battalions;[1] so there remained five British battalions (organized as two brigades) a brigade of field artillery, a field company R.E. a signal company, and two field ambulances.

An Allied Conference was held in London in February 1921 with a view to revising the Treaty of Sèvres, the terms of which were felt to be too severe on the Turks.[2] King Constantine, however, encouraged by the permission of the Supreme Council to land in Smyrna and then to advance from the enclave awarded to the Greeks by the Treaty of Sèvres, brought about a struggle by conceiving a plan for conquering Anatolia and restoring the old Constantinople (Byzantine) Empire. As if to flout the Conference, the Greeks – without any great success – attacked the Kemalists from their three holdings, the Smyrna area, Brusa and Ismid, and rejected the terms formulated by the Conference which the Turks had accepted. A raw Greek division,

---

[1] The Irish Guards, 2/Sherwood Foresters and 1/Loyal Regiment. The 2/Essex and 1/Buffs now relieved the Gordons and Hampshire; and the 3rd Hussars, the 20th Hussars; and the XIX. Brigade R.F.A., the X. Brigade R.F.A.

[2] Both the Constantinople Government and the Nationalists sent representatives, but they fused into one party. Italy took the opportunity to make a treaty with Turkey to withdraw her troops.

which had relieved a good one at Ismid so that the latter might join the Brusa force, was attacked by the Turks and fled, thus creating another liability for the Allies, who declared a neutral zone in front of their Ismid line.

On the 8th July the Greeks started on their advance towards Ankara, which could only lead them into a pocket, and at first did well; but in September, through lack of cavalry, being caught in the loop of the Sakaria river, south-east of Ankara, had to fall back; and both sides then settled down for the winter. In October the collision between the French and the Nationalist troops in Cilicia was brought to an end by the Treaty secretly negotiated at Ankara Monsieur Franklin-Bouillon, President of the Senate, which brought about the withdrawal of the French troops and, it was rumoured contained clauses guaranteeing the support of the Turkish claims to Thrace and Smyrna. A conference in Paris in March 1922 tried to arrange terms on the basis that the Greeks should evacuate Asia Minor and return certain territory in Thrace. Those terms were accepted by the Greeks, and G.H.Q. made preparations to supervise an evacuation; but Kemal rejected the terms.

GREEK THREAT TO CONSTANTINOPLE [1]

An astonishing event now (that is mid-July 1922) took place: the Greeks concentrated troops, estimated from 15,000 to 25,000 men, within four or five hours' march of the western boundary of the zone of allied occupation in Thrace, with, it was believed the intention of seizing Constantinople. General Harington informed them that it would be considered an hostile act if they crossed the neutral line which had been fixed. Arrangements were made to exert naval pressure on Athens, and the French, with the assistance of British troops, including all the cavalry and artillery from the Asiatic side, under command of General Charpy, manned the Chatalja lines. French reinforcements, too, of a cavalry regiment and a brigade of artillery arrived from Marseilles; but even then the lines, fifteen miles in length, were too long for the small international force to hold. This gave the Constantinople Turks an excuse for raising volunteers – became useful to them later. On the British Government approving General Harington's action, the Greeks Government disavowed any hostile action intention, and another Allied Conference was assembled, this time at Venice, to arrange a settlement.

DEFEAT OF THE GREEKS IN ANATOLIA

Such was the situation when, on 26th August, Kemal struck in Anatolia, and by the 18th September the Greek troops in Asia had either been killed, taken prisoner or driven out. There was nothing now between the Nationalists and Constantinople except a few British troops. General Harington on the 9th September telegraphed to the War Office that he had learnt by secret information that the Nationalists had the intention in a few days of menacing Chanak and Anatoli Hissar. He gave warning to them not to cross the neutral line, which he had marked by flags, and General Charpy and General Mombelli sent small forces to the Dardanelles and the Ismid front to show the solidarity of the Allies; the Greek community in Constantinople offered to furnish 7,000 old soldiers and 20,000 recruits, a gesture which was merely noted, as

---

[1] A full account of this incident will be found in the General Staff War Diary of the Allied Forces of Occupation, July 1922, started on the 17th of that month after having ceased in October 1920.

their employment might have caused more trouble with the Turks. By order of their respective Governments, however, the French and Italian contingents were soon withdrawn to Constantinople, but remained under General Harington's orders to maintain tranquillity there.

An Inter-Allied Commission, however, with an Italian colonel as president and British and French members, was sent to Bursa to prevent pillage and burning as far as possible, and to hand over to the Nationalist on their arrival. This mission was successfully accomplished.

The employment of the Turkish gendarmerie against the Nationalists was forbidden.

DEFENCE OF THE DARDENELLES: CHANAK [1]

General Harington realized that the Narrows of the Dardanelles at Chanak were the critical point; for if this passage were commanded by the Nationalists, it was barred to the Royal Navy, of which the Turks stood more in respect than of the soldiers; but he also felt assured that, if handled firmly, the Nationalists would not dare to "take on" the British Empire.

The War Office suggested that Chanak should be evacuated and the troops there transferred to Gallipoli. As it was not considered satisfactory that this place should be held by French and Italian troops alone, and ordered that Gallipoli and Constantinople should be held at all costs; but the capital could not be defended without holding Scutari and beyond.

Chanak was garrisoned by only one battalion, the 1/Loyal Regiment. General Harington decided to reinforce it at the expense of depleting his small force elsewhere. Field-Marshal Lord Plumer, Governor of Malta, who happened to be on a visit to his old chief General Staff officer, agreed with him. With his own hand, he wrote out a telegram to the War Office, giving the situation, and saying that he entirely approved of General Harington's plans.[2] He addressed a similar personal telegram to Mr. Lloyd George; and he ordered the 1/Gordon Highlanders and 2/R. Sussex from Malta. From Constantinople a squadron of the 3rd Hussars, a battery of artillery and the 2nd/Sherwood Foresters were dispatched; but the cavalry, moving by land, encountered a force of about three thousand mounted Turks, who forced it to retire, and it proceeded, with a battery, by water. The Navy sent three battleships, with cruisers and destroyers, under Rear-Admiral J. Kelly, who put seamen and Royal Marines ashore to aid in construction of a field position. The Mediterranean stations were denuded of their garrisons to furnish reinforcements: the 1/K.O.S.B., 2/Highland L.I., two batteries of the XVII. Brigade R.F.A., two batteries of the V. Pack Brigade, arrived from Egypt, and the III. Medium Brigade, in addition to two battalions already sent, from Malta. All those were assembled at Chanak by 26th September, when Major-General Marden was ordered by G.H.Q. to take over command from Br.-General D.I. Shuttleworth (83rd Brigade). He was instructed by General Harington to show a bold front; if attacked, to resist as long as possible and finally withdraw to Gallipoli, as evacuation was the policy of the Government. Soon afterwards No. 208 Squadron (Bristol Fighters) R.A.F. and a detached flight of No. 56 Squadron (Snipe) from Egypt appeared, and they were soon reinforced (11th – 17th October) by a headquarters staff and three squadrons No. 4 Squadron (Bristol Fighters), No. 25 Squadron (Snipe) and No. 207 Squadron (De.H. 9A's) from the United Kingdom, all under Group-Captain P.F.M. Fellowes; the 2/Grenadier Guards and 3/Coldstream Guards were on their way from the United Kingdom to form a Guards Brigade with the Irish Guards, already in Constantinople; a battalion of the Royal

---

[1] There is a good map in the war dairy for 18th – 20th September 1922.
[2] "Tim Harington Looks Back", p. 112.

Marine arrived there; 1/Duke of Wellington's and 1/South Staffordshire came from Gibraltar, and a brigade of R.F.A. from Egypt. The total force on the 18th October consisted of 15 infantry battalions,[1] with three 18-pdr. Batteries and six howitzer batteries (one 3,7-inch), of which the 83rd Brigade was on the Asiatic side, with headquarters at Haidar Pasha,[2] and the 84th and 85th Brigades at Chanak, with the two Guards Battalions from the United Kingdom on transports. Supported by the Navy (with three aircraft carriers) and R.A.F., so that the total air force was approximately 70 aircraft against a possible 50, the force would, no doubt, have given a good account of itself; but four brigades cannot defeat a whole nation in arms, and there were rumours that the Turks had acquired some drift mines, to dislodge the Navy.

THE MUDANIA CONVENTION

The Ismid front had remained quiet throughout this critical period; but by 1st October Nationalist forces – three cavalry divisions – had encircled Chanak. It was locally learnt that they had orders not to attack, and Kemal himself gave notice that no aggressive action was intended. In any case, Major-General Marden, with an airfield at Gallipoli, machine guns on the Gallipoli side, and most of the Mediterranean fleet, reinforced by units of the Atlantic fleet, in the Dardanelles, felt confident that with six battalions he could hold his position. General Harington's fear was that the Turks would now move against Constantinople, where he could assemble no more than another six battalions. Monsieur Franklin-Bouillon, however, was in touch with the Nationalist Government, seeking to persuade them to enter into negotiations to establish peace, and on the 1st October General Harington was informed that the Turks had agreed to a conference at Mudania (on the Sea of Marmora between Chanak and Constantinople).[3] The conference met on the 3rd October, the Allies being represented by the Directing Committee of Generals – Harington, Charpy and Mombelli – Turkey by Ismet Pasha, commanding the Armies on the Western front, and Greece by General Marakis and Colonel Sarriyanis. The discussions lasted over a week, until the 11th October, and even then the Greek delegates refused to sign the Convention.

The principle points agreed on by the other delegates, in the order given here were that hostilities between the Turkish and Hellenic troops should cease, and that the latter should evacuate Eastern Thrace and retire behind the Maritza; that the evacuation, including the retirement of the Greek civil officials, should be completed in 15 days; that it should be supervised by a mixed military commission, which might have the support of seven Allied battalions to maintain order; that the Turkish administration, with a force of gendarmerie limited to 8,000 men, would take over, the transfer being effected under the direction of the military commission; and that the commission and the Allied battalions should retire in thirty days, or sooner, after the completion of the evacuation of the Greek troops.

In Asia, demarcation lines, 15 kilometres from the Chanak shore and about 40 kilometres

---

[1] 1st Guards Brigade (Colonel-Commandant J.MC.C. Steele), 3 battalions,
83rd Brigade (Colonel-Commandant D.I. Shuttleworth), 4 battalions,
84th Brigade (Colonel-Commandant W.B. Emory), 4 battalions,
85th Brigade (Colonel-Commandant A.T. Beckwith), 4 battalions.
[2] On 25th September it came directly under G.H.Q.
[3] The whole story is related at length by General Harington in his "Tim Harington Looks Back", and by Major-General Sir Thomas Marden in his article "With the British Army in Constantinople. A Personal Narrative", in the *Army Quarterly*, July and October 1933.

from the base of the Ismid Peninsula, beyond which the Turkish troops were not to pass were defined, leaving them to be marked on the ground by a mixed contingent and which agreed not to increase the strength of their troops or to construct fortifications or military works in these two regions. The Allied troops might remain where they were, actually stationed on Turkish territory in the Constantinople and Gallipoli peninsulas until the decision of the Peace Conference.

The Turkish Government also engaged not to transport troops nor to raise or maintain an army in Eastern Thrace until the ratification of peace.

The Mudania Convention came into force three days later, at midnight 14th/15th October 1922.

THE PEACE TREATY OF LAUSANNE

The Conference at Lausanne to draw up a Peace Treaty between the Allies and Turkey did not assemble until the 29th November, and, although no incident occurred, the interval was a trying one for General Harington, as he estimated that 40,000 Nationalists could attack Chanak, and 50,000 could advance on Constantinople via Ismid, whilst there were 20,000 Turkish troops in the city itself, and the 8,000 gendarmerie in Thrace had swollen into at least 20,000 armed men, as the inhabitants were being organized. But the commanders of both sides had their troops in hand, and no unfortunate incident occurred.

The British Empire was represented at the Conference by the Marquess Curzon of Kedleston and Sir Horace Rumbold, the Ambassador at Constantinople.[1]

The critical time was greatly lengthened as the Turks proved difficult to deal with and threatened just before Christmas to put their Armies into motion again. On the 4th February 1923 the Turkish delegates left the Conference, it was not resumed until the 23rd April, and the Treaty was not signed until the 24th July 1923, and then only because the Turks found it difficult and expensive to keep large forces in the field, and the Greek Army, re-formed and re-organized behind Maritza, pretty plainly showed its intention of crossing the river and re-occupying Eastern Thrace. In negotiation there must be force to back the successful negotiator. General Pellé, the only soldier in the delegation, signed for France, and the Treaty was ratified at Ankara on the 23rd August.

By the Treaty of Lausanne, of 143 Articles, the Turkish Republic (the Sultan had been deposed in November 1921) regained Eastern Thrace and Smyrna which had been lost by the terms of the Treaty of Sèvres; the Zone of the Straits dropped out, but, by special conventions attached to the Treaty, demilitarised zones were instituted not only on both shores of the Straits, but on both sides of the new Greek and Bulgarian frontiers with Thrace. Instead of dealing solely with the ticklish military situation, endeavour was made to arrive at a "clean slate" with Turkey. Arrangements were included in the Treaty for exchange of populations and the protections of minorities; for distribution of the Ottoman Public Debt, in accordance with divisions of the territory of the old Turkish Empire; for a mixed Arbitral Tribunal to settle

---

[1] Major-General Sir Rudolph Slatin Pasha, an Austrian, once a prisoner of the Mahdi at Khartoum, and subsequently a major-general in the Anglo-Egyptian Army, told the complier that a great mistake had been made in the selection of the chief representative: he did not impress the Turks, who, seeing him clean-shaven and in a civilian frockcoat, thought he was a Court eunuch. "You should have sent a man with a big moustache in a Life Guards uniform".

questions of property, rights and interests of Allied nationals involved in the changes; also contracts and life insurance, debts, industrial, literary and artistic property; communications and sanitary questions, prisoners of war, graves and memorials. Turkey got back her captured ships, but did not receive the indemnity from Greece for which she held out.

EVACUATION

The evacuation of the Allied garrisons for which every preparation had been made, was begun on the day after ratification and was completed by the 2nd October. The final ceremony took place at 11.30 a.m. at Dolma Baghche Palace on the Bosphorus, and at 3 p.m. the last British transport left Constantinople.

The long delay before the first peace terms were presented to the Turks gave the Nationalists time to recover from disorder and shock of defeat; the small Army of Occupation made them contemptuous. The popular vote at an election which put Venizelos out of power had resulted to Greece in her complete defeat in the field, the loss of thousands of lives, and her deprivation of large areas of territory allotted to her by the Allies.

General View of Constantinople, 18 March 1920.
(IWM Q37441)

Constantinople from HMS Montrose 5 December 1919 (IWM Q37431)

The 28th Division landing at Constantinople with French Sailors looking on, November 1918. (IWM Q13870)

The 28th Division marching through the Streets of Constantinople, November 1918 (IWM Q13874)

Lieut.-General Sir Henry Maitland Wilson taking the Salute, Constantinople, 10 Novmber 1918 (IWM Q13864)

Released British Prisoners of War about to be Repatriated, November 1918, Constantinople (IWM Q13949)

General Franchet d'Esperey coming Ashore, Constantinople, 8 February 1919 (IWM Q13946)

General Franchet d'Esperey, with General Sir George Milne behind, taking the Salute, Constantinople, 8 February 1919. (IWM Q13947)

Round Up of Turkish Officials being guarded by the Royal Navy, Constantinople, (IWM Q113471)

The Entrance of the Arsenal, Constantinople, c1919. (IWM Q14269)

Interior of the Arsenal, Constantinople, c1919. Note the stacks of Rifles. (IWM Q14268)

General Sir Edmund Ironside (centre) and Staff, Constantinople, c1920. (IWM Q113473)

CONSTANTINOPLE

MAP: THE MEDITERRANEAN THEATRE

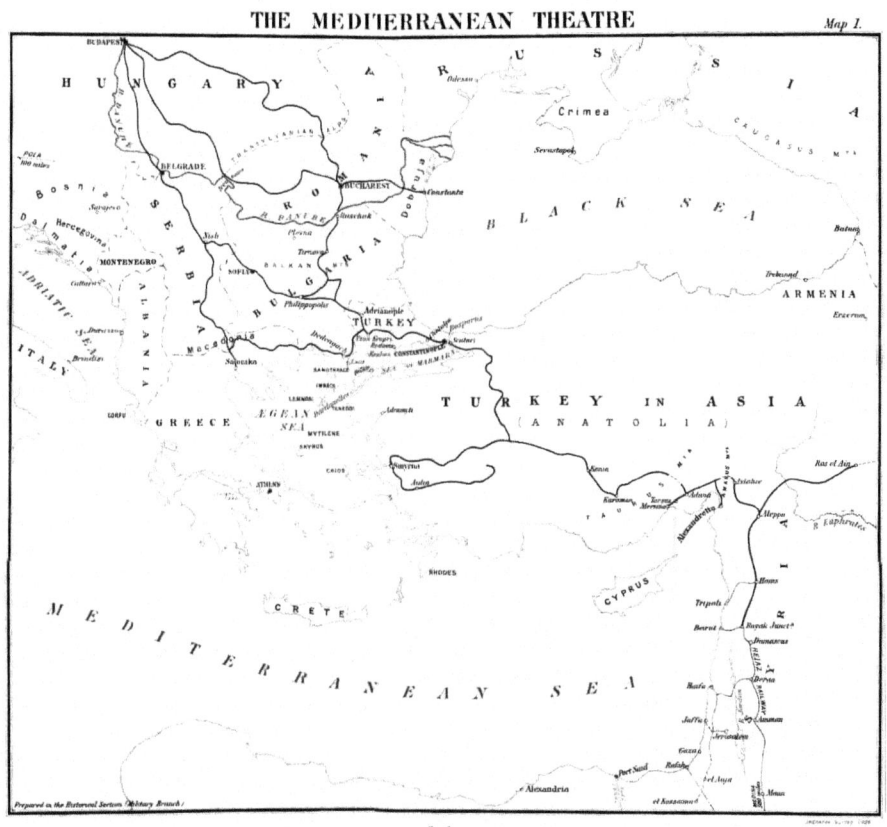

CONSTANTINOPLE

MAP: TURKEY IN EUROPE

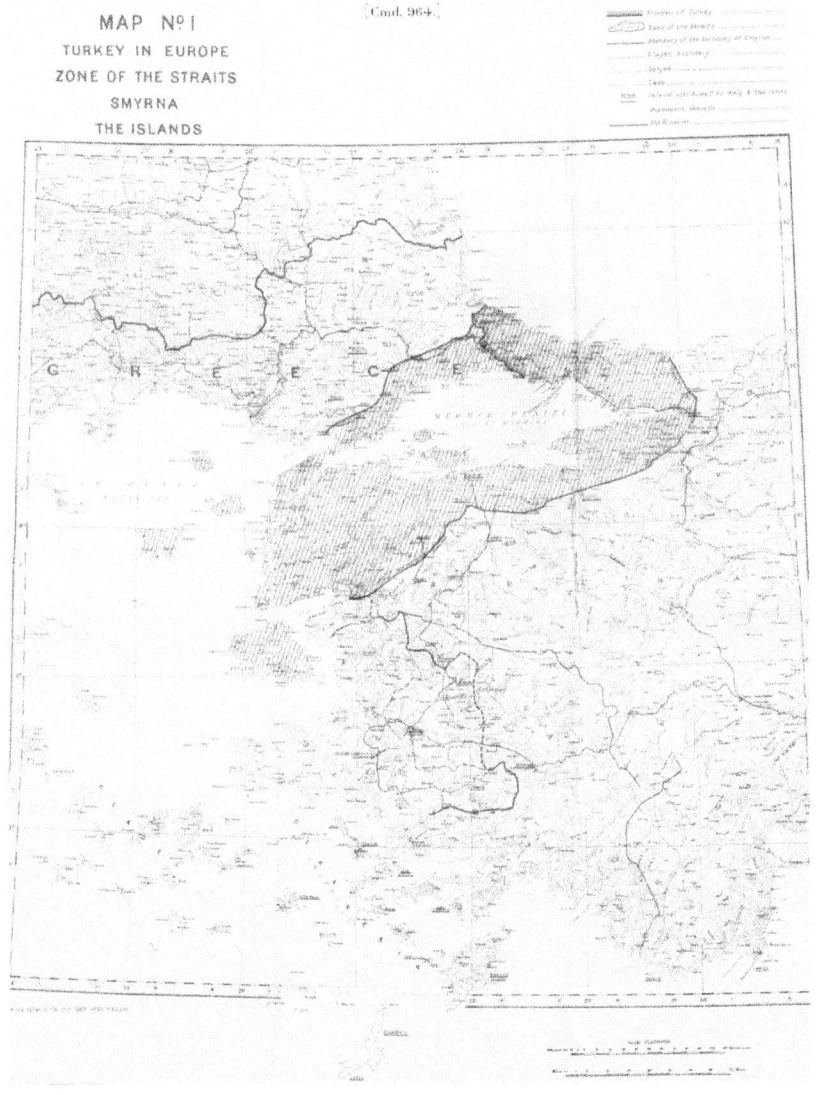

CONSTANTINOPLE

APPENDICES

APPENDIX I

THE TERMS OF THE ARMISTICE WITH TURKEY, 30TH OCTOBER, 1918

Conditions of an Armistice agreed to and concluded between –

Vice-Admiral the Honourable Sir Somerset Arthur Gough-Calthorpe, British Commander-in-Chief of the Mediterranean Station, acting under the authority from the British Government, in agreement with their Allies,

and

His Excellency Raouf Bey, Turkish Minister of Marine; His Excellency Rechad Hikmet Bey, Turkish Under-Secretary for Foreign Affairs; Lieutenant-Colonel Saadullah Bey, Turkish General Staff; acting under authority from the Turkish Government.

1. Opening of Dardanelles and Bosphorus and secure access to the Black Sea. Allied occupation of Dardanelles and Bosphorus forts.

2. Positions of all minefields, torpedo-tubes, and other obstructions in Turkish waters to be indicated, and assistance given to sweep or remove them as may be required.

3. All available information as to mines in the Black Sea to be communicated.

4. All Allied prisoners of war and Armenian interned persons and prisoners to be collected in Constantinople and handed over unconditionally to the Allies.

5. Immediate demobilization of the Turkish Army, except for such troops as are required for surveillance of frontiers and for the maintenance of internal order. Number of effectives and their dispositions to be determined later by the Allies after consultation with the Turkish Government.

6. Surrender of all war vessels in Turkish waters, or in waters occupied by Turkey. These ships to be interned at such Turkish port or ports as may be directed, except such vessels as are required for police or similar purposes in Turkish territorial waters.

7. The Allies to have the right to occupy any strategic points in the event of any situation arising which threatens the security of the Allies.

8. Free use by the Allied ships of all ports and anchorages now in Turkish occupation, and denial of their use by enemy. Similar conditions to apply to Turkish mercantile shipping in Turkish waters for the purposes of trade and demobilization of the Army.

APPENDIX I

9. Use of all ship repair facilities at all Turkish ports and arsenals.

10. Allied occupation of the Taurus tunnel system.

11. Immediate withdrawal of Turkish troops from North-west Persia to behind the pre-war frontier has already been ordered, and will be carried out. Part of Trans Caucasia has already been ordered to be evacuated by Turkish troops; the remainder to be evacuated if required by the Allies after they have studied the situation there.

12. Wireless-telegraph and cable stations to be controlled by the Allies, Turkish Government messages excepted.

13. Prohibition to destroy any naval, military, or commercial material.

14. Facilities to be given for the purchase of coal, oil-fuel, and naval material from Turkish sources after the requirements of the country have been met. None of the above material to be exported.

15. Allied Control Officers to be placed on all railways, including such portions of the Trans-Caucasian railways now under Turkish control, which must be placed at the free and complete disposal of the Allied authorities, due consideration being given to the needs of the population. This clause to include Allied occupation of Batum. Turkey will raise no objection to the occupation of Baku by the Allies.

16. The surrender of all garrisons in Hejaz, Assir, Yemen, Syria, and Mesopotamia to the nearest Allied Commander and the withdrawal of troops from Cilicia, except those necessary to maintain order, as will be determined under Clause 5.

17. Surrender of all Turkish officers in Tripolitania and Cyrenaica to the nearest Italian garrison. Turkey guarantees to stop supplies and communication with these officers if they do not obey the order to surrender.

18. Surrender of all ports occupied in Tripolitania and Cyrenaica, including Misurata, to the nearest Allied garrison.

19. All Germans and Austrians, naval, military and civilian, to be evacuated within one month from Turkish dominions. Those in remote districts as soon after as may be possible.

20. Compliance with such orders as may be conveyed for the disposal of the equipment, arms, and ammunition, including transport, of that portion of the Turkish Army which is demobilized under Clause 5.

21. An Allied representative to be attached to the Turkish Ministry of Supplies in order to safeguard Allied interests. This representative to be furnished with all information necessary for this purpose.

22. Turkish prisoners to be kept at the disposal of the Allied Powers. The release of Turkish civilian prisoners and prisoners over military age to be considered.

23. Obligation on part of Turkey to cease all relations with the Central Powers.

24. In case of disorder in the six Armenian vilayets the Allies reserve to themselves the right to occupy any part of them.

25. Hostilities between the Allies and Turkey shall cease from noon, local time on Thursday, 31st October, 1918.

Signed in duplicate on board His Majesty's ship *Agamennon*, at Port Mudros, Lemnos, the 30th October, 1918.

APPENDIX IIa

THE MILITARY INTER-ALLIED COMMISSION OF CONTROL AND ORGANIZATION

Circular Memorandum.

The object of this memorandum is to the three Allied Corps of Occupation the objects for which the military Inter-Allied Commission of Control and Organization has been set up and the work it performs.

1. By agreement between the Allied Governments, the Military Inter-Allied Commission of Control and Organization has been set up with the object of ensuring the disarmament and the carrying out of the control and organization of the armed forces of Turkey, consequent on the Armistice Convention of October 30th, 1918 of performing such other duties as may be laid upon it from time to time by the Allied Governments. It has been set up as a provisional measure and functions without prejudice to any machinery which may be established by any treaty of peace which any subsequently be ratified between the Allied powers and Turkey.

2. The Military Inter-Allied Commission of Control and Organization is directed by the Directing Committee of Generals, consisting of a French, an Italian and a British Member, the last being President. The Directing Committee has delegated certain executive functions of the Military Inter-Allied Commission of Control and Organization to the following Sub-Commissions: -
    a. The Inter-Allied Sub-commission of Disarmament, consisting of a French, a British and an Italian member, the latter being President. The functions of this Sub-commission are to deal with questions regarding the control and disposal of Ottoman war material.
    b. The Inter-Allied Sub-commission of Gendarmerie, consisting of a British, an Italian and a French member, the latter being President. The functions of this Sub-commission are: -
    (i) to organise and control the existing Ottoman Gendarmerie and
    (ii) to study the future organisation of the gendarmerie force for the benefit of Turkey after the ratification of a peace treaty.
    c. The Inter-Allied Sub-commission of Special Elements, consisting of an Italian, a French and a British member, the last being President. Its functions are: -
    (i) to superintend the reorganization of the Ottoman War Office,
    (ii) to superintend the execution of military orders by the Ottoman War Office, with the exception of those concerning Gendarmerie and Disarmament which will be supervised by the sub-commission concerned,

though within the precincts of the Ottoman War Office the actual supervision is carried out by the Inter-Allied Liaison Section acting as representative of the various Sub-commissions,
(iii) to superintend the employment of the few Turkish Regular units which exist under the orders of the Central Government,
(iv) to co-operate with the Sub-commission of Gendarmerie and Disarmament regarding certain requirements and
(v) to study problems concerned with the Turkish Regular Army of the future.

3. The Directing Committee of Generals has at the same time set up the Inter-Allied Liaison Section, Ottoman War Office, consisting of an Italian, a French and a British member, the last being President. This section has no executive powers. Its duties are: -
(i) to act as the channel of communication between the President of the Directing Committee of Generals or any of the Sub-commissions and the Minister of War and regarding certain questions, to communicate through the latter with the Minister of the Interior.
(ii) to supervise the execution within the Ottoman War Office of all orders or instructions given by the President of the Directing Committee of Generals or any of the Sub-commissions and
(iii) to supply to them all information it may obtain.
Each member of this section represents the particular Sub-commission which is under the presidency of an officer of his nationality.
The section is at the same time the military representative of the Allied Command and carries out the above-described functions on behalf of the General Officer Commanding-in-Chief, the Allied Forces of Occupation, when required.

4. The normal channels of communication between the various commands and commissions and the Turkish authorities are shown in the attached diagram. (not reproduced)

The orders of the Presidents of the Sub-commissions to the Turkish Minister of War are addressed direct, but actually passed as shown in the diagram through the Inter-Allied Liaison Section. The same channel is used when the Ottoman Minister of War wishes to communicate with General Headquarters, the Allied Forces of Occupation, or the Sub-commissions.

Communications between Corps commanders and the Presidents of the Sub-commissions, and vice versa, is direct as shown.

General Headquarters,
The Allied Forces of
Occupation (Turkey).

(signed) W.H. Gribbons
Colonel on the Staff,
General Staff.

APPENDIX IIb

COMPOSITION AND LOCATION OF THE MILITARY INTER-ALLIED COMMISSION OF CONTROL AND ORGANIZATION

3rd Bureau
CR.AF/1161/3

March 24th, 1922.

The Directing Committee of Generals

President and British Member,	Lieutenant-General Sir Charles H. HARINGTON, K.C.B., D.S.O.
Italian Member,	Général de Division E. MOMBELLI, K.C.M.G.
French Member,	Major-General C. CHARPY, C.B.
Secretary,	Lieutenant-Colonel T.G.G. HEYWOOD, O.B.E.
Offices,	General Headquarters, the Allied Forces of Occupation, NISHANTASH.

The Inter-Allied Sub-commission of Disarmament

President and Italian Member, Major-General BASSIONANO.
French Member, Lieutenant-General CHATEL.
British Member, Lieutenant-General W.C.E. TWIDALE, C.M.G., D.S.O.
Secretary, Lieutenant MARTINENGO.
Offices, Ottoman War Office.

The Inter-Allied Sub-commission of Gendarmerie

President and French Member,	Major-General FILLONNEAU, C.M.G.
Italian Member,	Colonel CAPRINI.
British Member,	Lieutenant-General J.A.W. SPENCER, C.M.G, D.S.O.
Secretary,	Lieutenant WURTZ.
Offices,	Headquarters, Ottoman Gendarmerie.

The Inter-Allied Sub-commission of Special Elements.

President and British Member,	Major-General G. McK. FRANKS, C.B.
Italian Member,	Colonel MONTAGANO.
French Member,	Commandant GENIN.
Secretary,	
Offices,	Ottoman War Office.

CONSTANTINOPLE

The Inter-Allied Liaison Section, Ottoman War Office.

President and British Member,	Colonel A.T. BECKWITH, C.B., C.M.G., D.S.O.
Italian Member,	Colonel MONTAGANO.
French Member,	Commandant LAYER.
Secretary,	Captain G.E. WHEELER.
Offices,	Ottoman War Office.

APPENDIX III

**TREATY SERIES
TRIPARTITE AGREEMENT
BETWEEN
BRITISH EMPIRE, FRANCE AND ITALY
RESPECTING
ANATOLIA
SIGNED AT SÈVRES AUGUST 10TH, 1920.**

Being anxious to help Turkey to develop her resources and avoid international rivalries.

Art. 1. "There shall be perfect equality in Turkey in the composition of all international commissions whether existing or to be established (including the different services dependent thereon)".

Art. 4. "The Anatolian railway and that part of the Baghdad railway which lies in Turkish territory shall be worked by a company whose capital will be subscribed by British, French and Italian financial groups".

Art. 5. Defines spheres of influence: after cutting off the "Zone of the Straits" and the territory of Smyrna Italy has the South-West and France the South-East, leaving the north belt to the British.

Art. 6. Deals with rights in mandated territories.

Art. 7. Re the coal basin of Heraclea.

Art. 8. Prescribes that France and Italy shall withdraw troops in to their own spheres.

Art. 9. Prescribes that each contracting Power shall accept responsibility for supervising the execution of the Treaty of Peace with regards to minorities.

Art. 10. Arranges that the agreement is to come in to force at the same time as the Treaty of Peace does.

APPENDIX IV

TREATY OF PEACE WITH TURKEY SIGNED AT SÈVRES 10TH AUGUST, 1920 (UNRATIFIED).

Part I
(Articles 1-26): Repeats the Covenant of the League of Nations.

Part II
(Articles 27-35): Gives the Frontiers of Turkey.

Part III
(Articles 36-139): Is headed "Political Clauses". The articles of historical interest are 37-64 which, under the heading "Straits", create a Commission, "in complete independence of the local authority" to control the navigation of the Dardanelles, Sea of Marmora and Bosphorus, with its own flag and budget. The Commissioners of U.S.A., British Empire, France, Italy and Russia (if a member of the League of Nations) were to have 2 votes, the 4 small nations concerned, one only. The Chairmanship was to be rotatory and for 2 years, among the Commissioners entitled to 2 votes.

Other articles dealt with Smyrna, Greece, Armenia, Syria, Mesopotamia, Palestine, Hedjez, Egypt, Sudan, Cyprus, Morocco, Tunis, Lybia, Ægean Islands.

Part IV
(Articles 140-151): Deals with the Protection of Minorities.

Part V
(Articles 152-207): Military, Naval and Air clauses, laid down to what extent Turkey was to be disarmed and what forces she might keep up, also the educational establishments, Customs Officials, local urban and rural police, forest guards.

(Articles 196-205): They legislated for three Commissions of Control, Military, Naval and Air and are here given in full.

APPENDIX IV

Inter-Allied Commissions of Control and Organization.
Article 196.

Subject to any special provisions in this Part, the military, naval and air clauses contained in the present treaty shall be executed by Turkey and at her expense under the control of Inter-Allied Commissions appointed for this purpose by the Principal Allied Powers.

The above-mentioned Commissions will represent the Principal Allied Powers in dealing with the Turkish Government in all matter relating to the execution of the military, naval and air clauses. They will communicate to the Turkish authorities the decisions which the Principal Allied Powers have reserved the right to take, or which the execution of the said clauses may necessitate.

Article 197.

The Inter-Allied Commissions of Control and Organization may establish their organisations at Constantinople, and will be entitled, as often as they think desirable, to proceed to any point whatever in Turkish territory, or to send sub-commissions, or to authorise one or more of their members to go, to any such point.

Article 198.

The Turkish Government must furnish to the Inter-Allied Commissions of Control and Organization all such information and documents as the latter may deem necessary for the accomplishment of their mission, and must supply at its own expense all labour and materials which the said Commissions may require in order to ensure the complete execution of the military, naval and air clauses.

The Turkish Government shall attach a qualified representative to each Commission for the purpose of receiving all communications which the Commission may have to address to the Turkish Government, and of supplying or procuring for the Commission all information or documents which may be required.

Article 199.

The upkeep and cost of the Inter-Allied Commissions of Control and Organization and the expense incurred by their work shall be borne by Turkey.

Article 200.

The Military Inter-Allied Commission of Control and Organization will be entrusted on one hand with the supervision of the execution of the military clauses relating to the reduction of the Turkish forces within the authorised limits, the delivery of arms and war material prescribed in Chapter VI of Section I, and the disarmament of the fortified regions prescribed in Chapters VII and VIII of that Section, and on the other hand with the organization and the control of the employment of the new Turkish armed force.

(1) As the Military Inter-Allied Commission of Control it will be its special duty:

(a) to fix the number of customs officials, local urban and rural police, forest guards and other like officials which Turkey will be authorised to maintain in accordance with Article 170;

(b) to receive from the Turkish Government the notifications relating to the location of the stocks and depots of munitions, the armaments of the fortified works, fortress and forts, the situation of the works or factories for the production of arms, munitions and war material and their operations;

(c) to take delivery of the arms, munitions and war material and plant intended for manufacture of the same, to select the points where such delivery is to be effected, and to supervise the works of rendering things useless and of conversion provided for by the present Treaty.

(2) As the Military Inter-Allied Commission of Organization it will be its special duty:
(a) to proceed, in collaboration with the Turkish Government, with the organization of the Turkish armed force upon the basis laid down in Chapter I to IV, Section I of this Part, with the delimitation of the territorial regions provided for in Article 156, and with the distribution of troops of gendarmerie and the special elements for reinforcement between different territorial regions;
(b) to control the condition for the employment, as laid down in Articles 156 and 157, of these troops of gendarmerie and the elements, and to decide what effect shall be given to requests of the Turkish Government for the provisional modification of normal distribution of these forces determined in conformity with said Articles;
(c) to determined the proportion by nationality of the Allied and neutral officers to be engaged to serve in the Turkish gendarmerie under the conditions laid down in Article 159, and to lay down the conditions under which they are to participate in the different duties provided for them in the said Article.

Article 201.

It will be the special duty of the Naval Inter-Allied Commission of Control to visit the building yards and to supervise the breaking up of the ships, to take delivery of the arms, munitions and naval war material and to supervise their destruction and breaking up.

The Turkish Government must furnish to the Naval Inter-Allied Commission of Control all such information and documents as the latter may deem necessary to ensure the complete execution of the naval clauses, in particular the design of the warships, the composition of their armaments, the details and models of the guns, munitions, torpedoes, mines, explosives, wireless telegraphic apparatus and in general everything relating to naval war material, as well as all legislative or administrative documents and regulations.

Article 202.

It will be the special duty of the Aeronautical Inter-Allied Commission of Control to make an inventory of the aeronautical material now in the hands of the Turkish Government, to inspect aeroplanes, balloon and motor manufactories and factories producing arms, munitions and explosives capable of being used by aircraft, to visit all aerodromes, sheds, landing grounds, parks and depots on Turkish territory, to arrange, if necessary, for the removal of material and to take delivery of such material.

The Turkish Government must furnish to the Aeronautical Inter-Allied Commission of Control all such information and legislative, administrative or other documents as the Commission may consider necessary to ensure the complete execution of the air clauses, in particular a list of the personnel belonging to all the Turkish air services and of the existing material as well as of that in process of manufacture or on order, and a complete list of all establishments working for aviation, of their positions, and of all sheds and landing grounds.

APPENDIX IV

Article 203.

The Military, Naval and Aeronautical Inter-Allied Commissions of Control will appoint representatives who will jointly responsible for controlling the execution of the operations provided for in paragraphs (1) and (2) of Article 178.

Article 204.

Pending the definitive settlement of the political status of the territories referred to in Article 89, the decisions of the Inter-Allied Commissions of Control and Organization will be subject to any modifications which the said Commissions may consider necessary in consequence of such settlement.

Article 205.

The Naval and Aeronautical Inter-Allied Commission of Control will cease to operate on the completion of the tasks assigned to them respectively by Article 201 and 202.

The same will apply to the section of the Military Inter-Allied Commission of Control entrusted with the functions of control prescribed in Article 200 (1).

The section of the said Commission entrusted with the organization of the new Turkish armed force as provided in Article 200 (2) will operate for five years from the coming into force of the present Treaty. The Principal Allied Powers reserve the right to decide, at the end of this period, whether it is desirable to maintain or suppress this section of the said Commission.

The remaining articles concern Prisoners of War, Graves, Penalties, Finance, Economic matters, Aerial Navigation, Ports, Waterways, Railways, Labour.

APPENDIX V

JURISDICTION AND MAINTENANCE OF LAW AND ORDER IN CONSTANTINOPLE, 8TH SEPTEMBER, 1921.
ORDER BY
LIEUTENANT-GENERAL SIR CHARLES HARINGTON, K.C.B., D.S.O.
COMMANDING-IN-CHIEF.
ALLIED FORCES OF OCCUPATION.

WHEREAS some time past the British Military Forces have by virtue of their inherent rights of occupation tried and punished offences committed by the civilian population against the interest and safety of the British Army and against public law and order in Constantinople.

And WHEREAS the prolongation of a state of war under an Armistice between the Allied Powers on the one part and Turkey on the other has rendered it desirable that the civilian population shall be informed of the methods whereby the maintenance of law and order in Constantinople has been and will continue to be obtained.

Now therefore I, the undersigned, being the General Officer Commanding Allied Forces of Occupation Constantinople do hereby direct that the existing tribunals shall continue to exercise the functions which they have heretofore exercised by virtue of the occupation of Constantinople by the Allied Powers in the area of Pera and Galata, that is to say:-

The tribunals referred to in para. 1 hereof will continue to administer penal justice in the "NAME OF THE LAW" subject to the following regulations:-

(1) The tribunals are as follows:-
   (a) Magisterial Courts consisting of one Magisterial Officer having power to deal with offences and to inflict punishments of 28 days Imprisonment with or without Hard Labour or a fine not exceeding Lt. 50.
   (b) Provost Courts consisting of two Magisterial Officers or one Magisterial Officer, with another Officer appointed under my authority, and having power to punish offences by the award of 6 months Imprisonment with or without Hard Labour or a fine not exceeding Lt. 400.
   (c) Military Courts constituted in accordance with the custom of the service of the British Army and consisting of 3 Officers sitting either with or without a Judge Advocate and having power to award a sentence of Imprisonment with or without Hard Labour or Death subject to my confirmation.

(2) No French or Italian Subjects shall be tried by any of these tribunals.

(3) The powers of His Britannic Majesty's Supreme Court for the Ottoman Dominions are unaffected by the terms of this Order.

APPENDIX V

(4) These tribunals shall have jurisdiction over:-
(a) All British Subjects in the occupied territory of Turkey who commit offences against the interest and safety of the Allied Armies.
(b) All Allied Subjects with the exception of those mentioned in para. 2 hereof.
(c) All neutral subjects whose State has not established a Consular Court or who have not the benefit of the Capitulations.
(d) All Ottoman Subjects who commit offences against Allied Subjects.
(e) All Ottoman Subjects who infringe the regulations of the Allied Police Commission.
(f) All persons except those mentioned in para. (2) hereof, who shall commit offences which in my opinion are more properly dealt with by one of the tribunals set out herein.
(g) All persons of whatsoever nationality, except those mentioned in para. (2) hereof, who shall commit offences against the interests and safety of the British Army.

(5) No appeal shall be made from the decisions of the Military Court nor shall any appeal be made from the decisions of the other tribunals without the consent of such tribunals.

(6) The code of procedure shall be the same as a Field General Court-Martial.

(7) All offences shall be punished in accordance with the Ottoman Penal Code or the Regulations of the Inter-Allied Military Authorities or the Allied Police Commission. In the case of offences under the Ottoman Penal Code the maximum fine therein laid down may be increase 10 fold and shall be paid upon a gold basis.

(8) An accused person shall be given an opportunity of making his defence either in person or by Counsel recognised by the tribunal in question as by a person possessing the necessary qualifications of an advocate.

(9) All sentences of Imprisonment of the tribunals will be executed by the Allied Police Commission and served in such prisons as I shall think fit to order. Fines may be levied by distraint.

(10) All petitions from the decisions of any tribunal either upon law or fact shall be address to the Legal Officer Allied Forces of Occupation (Constantinople), who will lay this before me and my decision shall be final.

Signed at Constantinople this 8th day of September, 1921.

C. H. Harington.
LIEUTENANT-GENERAL,
COMMANDING-IN-CHIEF,
ALLIED FORCES OF OCCUPATION (CONSTANTINOPLE).

APPENDIX VI

ARMY OF THE BLACK SEA
STATISTICS OF ORDER OF BATTLE, SEPTEMBER, 1920.

(iii) September, 1920 (the last month but one, last available, under General Sir George Milne)

G.H.Q.

G.O.C. in C., Assistant Military Secretary and 2 A d. C	4
General Staff	11
Attached (Education)	2
Intelligence Branch Crimea	4
Special Service	5
A.G's Branch (including Br.General in charge of Administration)	6
Q.M.G's Branch	4
R.E. Services	6
Railway Directorate	7
Supply and Transport	3
Medical Services	6
Ordinance Services	7
Barrack Services	4
Special Appointments (Signals, A.P.M., Labour, Garrison Adjutant and Graves)	6
Requisitions and Hirings	3

Headquarters Allied Corps

G.O.C. and 2 A d. C	3
General Staff	3
A. & Q., and Medical	4

Chanak Base

D.A.P.M.	1

Constantinople Base

Commandant and Staff	5
Landing officers	6
Ordinance, Claims and Medical	3
Waterways and Docks	3

APPENDIX VI

Turkish Police Control

Officers 13

Troops

28th Division
242nd Brigade

II. 1921 (After reduction on arrival of General Sir Charles Harington)

G.H.Q.

G.O.C. in C., Assistant Military Secretary and 2 A d. C	4
General Staff	10
Attached	2
Intelligence Branch Crimea	7
A.G's Branch (including Br.General in charge of Administration)	6
Q.M.G's Branch	2
R.E. Services	6
Railway Directorate	3
Supply and Transport	3
Medical Services	5
Ordinance Services	5
Barrack Services	4
Special Appointments (Signals, A.P.M., Labour, and Graves)	5

Chanak Base

D.A.P.M. 1

Constantinople Base

Staff	5
Landing officers	6
Ordinance, Claims and Medical	3
Waterways and Docks	2

Turkish Police Control

Officers 12

Troops

28th Division

CONSTANTINOPLE

INDEX

Ægean Sea	3
Administration, Inter-Allied Sanitary	7
Administration, Turkish	27
Admiralty, British	5
Admiralty, Turkish	12
Adrianople	3,13
Aeroplanes, German	17
Affairs, International	20
Afion Kara Hissar	17
Afium Kara Hissar	9,10
Agreement, Tripartite	8,17
Agreement, Turkey and Soviet Russia	11
Akbash, Fort of	11
Alliance rifts	13
Allenby, General Sir Edmund	2,5,9
Allies	1,2,11,13,17,19,25,26,27,29
Ambassador, British (Constantinople)	18.21,28
Anatoli Hissar	25
Anatolia	10,11,17,23,24,25
Ankara	9,11,25,28
Arbitral Tribunal	25
Armenia	8,16
Armenians	5,10
Armenian vilayets	2
Armies, Turkish Ottoman	1
Armistice, between Germany and the Allies	4
Armistice, between Turkish Nationalists and the Allies	13
Armistice, between Turkey and the Allies	1,2,3,4,6,8,9,11,13,16
Armistice, Article 1.	2
Armistice, Article 5.	2
Armistice, Article 7.	2,4
Armistice, Article 12.	2
Armistice, Article 15.	2,8
Armistice, Article 20.	2
Armistice, Article 24.	2
Armistice, Articles 57-61	16
Armistice, Articles 65-63	16
Armistice, Articles 196-205	16
Armistice, Articles 152-207	16
Armistice, terms	6
Arms, Hellenic	17
Army, British (Constantinople)	27 fn
Army Division, Greek	18
Army Divisions, British	1
Army Divisions, Indian	1
Army, Greek	6
Army List, Prussian	19
Army of Occupation, Allied	16
Athens	19,25
Atrocities	23 fn
Asia	25,27
Asia Minor	6,8,10,13,18,19,23,24,25
Baku	5
Balfour Line	17
Balkans	5
Balkan, Countries	6
Balkan, theatre of war	2
Banks, Austro-Hungarian	8
Banks, German	8
Battalions, Allied	27
Batum	3,5,10,18
Batum, Inter-allied Force	10
Batum, Military Governor	10
Bassionano, Major-General	23
Bechwith, Colonel A.T.	24
Berthelet, Général	6
Berlin	1
Bodyguard, Sultan's	16
Bolshevists, Russian	20
Bosphorus	4,6,11
Bostandjik	15

Boundary, Bulgarian-Turkish	3	Committee, Directing of Generals	21,22,23,24,27
Boxer Expedition, 1900	19		
Bridges, Lieut.-General G.T.M.	1,6	Committee, Inter-Allied	12
Britain	1	Committee, Enquiry	23
British	6,7,8,9	Committee, Prisoners of War Reception	8
Bristol Fighter	26	Commission, Arbitral	22
Brusa	9,13,24	Commission, Armenia and its Boundaries Arbitration	22
Bulgaria	1,16		
Bunoust, Général	4	Commission, Control, Allied	24
		Commission, Control and Organization	21
Caliphate	10	Commission, Control and Organization, Military Inter-Allied	23
Canteen, Expeditionary Force	7		
Captains of the Port, Inter-Allied	7	Commission, Financial	21,22
Caspian Sea	5	Commission, High	20
Caucasia	5	Commission, British High, Rhineland	6 fn
Caucasus	5,6	Commission of Control, Allied	12
Central Powers	1	Commission, Financial	6,16
Chargé d'affaires, Turkish	1	Commission, French and British Directors of Railways	8
Chanak	4,15,25,26,27,28		
Charpy, General	19,25,27	Commission, Inter-Allied	8,26
Chatalja	24,25	Commission, Inter-Allied Armistice	7 fn, 8
Chekmedje	15	Commissions, Control and Organization, Inter-Allied	16,21
Chief of the Imperial General Staff, British (CIGS)	18,21		
		Commission, Free Zone of Smyrna Boundary	22
Chief of the General Staff, Turkish	11		
China	19	Commission, Greece Boundary	22
Cicilia	5	Commission, International	16
Clauses, Financial	16	Commission, International Police	7
Coadjutors, French	6	Commission, Kurdistan	22
Coadjutors, Italian	6	Commission, Kurdistan Boundary	22
Columns, Allied	14	Commission, Juridical	6,22
Commander of the Allied Forces, British	21	Commission, Maritza	22
Commanders, Allied	2,12,13	Commission, Naval	21
Commanders, Senior French	20	Commission, Prison	7
Commanders, Senior Italian	20	Commission, The Straits	16,22
Commander-in- Chief, Allied	13,18,19,20,21,22	Commission, Smyrna Territory Boundary	22
		Commission, Syria and Mesopotamia Boundary	22
Commander-in-Chief, British	19,21		
Commander-in-Chief, British Naval	1	Commission, Zone of the Straits Boundary	22
Commander-in-Chief to the High Commissioners	20		
		Commissioner, High, Constantinople	2
Committee, Allied Military of Versailles	21	Commissioner, British High	6,7,11,13
Committee, Chiefs Of Staff	8	Commissioners, High	6,7,8,19,20.23
Committee, Control and Organization	24 fn	Commissioners, French High	20

54

INDEX

Commissioners, Italian High	20	De Haviland D.H. 9	13
Conference, Allied, Venice	25	De Haviland D.H. 9A	13,16
Conference, Lausanne	28	Delegates, British	16
Conference, Mudania	27	Delegates, French	16
Conference, Paris March 1922	25	Delegates, Italian	16
Conference, Peace	10,28	Delegates, Greek	427
Conference, Versailles	3	Delegates, Turkish	28
Congress, 1st Turkish Nationalist	10	Delegation, Turkish	16
Congress, 2nd Turkish Nationalist	10	Department, Control	12
Constantine, Greek King	19,24	Department, General Staff	12
Constantinople 3,4,5,6,7,8,9,10,11,12,13,14, 15,17,18,19,20,21,23,24,25,26,27,29,29		Department, Inspection of Arms and Ammunition	12
Consulate, Greek, Constantinople	4	Department, Intendance	12
Convention, Mudania	27	Department, Organization	12
Control Officers, Allied	2	Department, Recruiting	12
Cooke-Collis, Br.-General J.N.	10	Derindje	11,14
Corps, Allied	11,14	Diary, General Staff War (Allied Forces of Occupation)	25 fn
Corps, Inter-Allied	19		
Cory, Major-General Sir George	5 fn	Diplomatic Representatives, British (Greece and Switzerland)	1
Cot, General	11		
Council, Army	22	Djemal Pasha	10,11
Council, Allied Army (for British affairs)	20	Djevad Pasha	11
Council, Supreme	10,12,13,17,21,24	Duncan, Major-General Sir John	3,5 fn
Council, Supreme War	6		
Court, Inter-Allied	8	Egypt	13,16,18,26
Court, Inter-Allied Military	7,14	Elections, Greek	19
Courts, Turkish	7	Emissaries, Turkish	1
Crimea	6,19	Embassy, British, Constantinople	6
Crimes	7	Embassy, Greek, Constantinople	4
Criminals, Turkish War	16	Empire, British	16,17,19 fn,26,28
Croker, Major-General H.L.	4	Empire, Constantinople (Byzantine)	24
Curzon, Marques of Kedleston	28	Empire, Ottoman	13,17
Customs Officials, Turkish	16	Empire, Turkish	28
Cyprus	16	Entente Offensive	1
		Entente Powers	1,10
Damascus	1	Enver Pasha, Minister of War, Turkish	1,6
Danube	3	Erzeroum	9,10
Dardanelles	3,4,8,9,11,14,16,18,25,26	Eskishehr	9,10,12,17
Dardanelles, Asiatic side	8	Eunuch, Court	28 fn
Debt, Ottoman (Turkish) National	16	Europe	6,8,19
Debt, Ottoman (Turkish) Public	28	Evacuation	29
Dede Agach	3		
Defences, Turkish (Bosphorus)	3	Fellowes, Group-Captain P.F.M.	26
Defences, Turkish (Dardanelles)	3	Fillonneau, Major-General	23

Fleet, Atlantic	27	Gay, Major-General A.W.	3
Fleet, Mediterranean	27	Gendarmerie, Greek	20
Foch, Maréchal F.	6,18	Gendarmerie, Macedonian	7,21
Force, Allied	18	Gendarmerie, Turkish	
Force, British	18	7,12,16,17,20,21,23,26,27	
Force, French	15,18	Generals, French	20
Force, Greek Brusa	25	Generals, Italian	20
Force, Italian	18	G.H.Q., (General Headquarters)	
Force, Palestine	9	British	3,4,6,12,17,19,25,26
Forces, Allied	5,6,7,12,14,18	G.H.Q., French, Guard	11
Forces, Turkish Armed	14,16,19	G.O.C., (General Officer Commanding)	
Forces, Turkish Nationalist	12,23,27	28th Division	14
Forces, Hellenic (Greek)	13,17,23	G.O.C., 85th Brigade	14
Foreign Minister, Turkish	5	G.O.C., Allied Forces	20
Foreign Ministry, Turkish	3 fn	G.O.C., Allies Forces, Gallipoli and	
Foreign Office, British	5,6,22,18 fn	Bosphorus	3
Forestier-Walker, Major-General		G.O.C., Army of the Black Sea	7
Sir George	5	G.O.C., French Contingent	15
Forts, Asiatic (Turkish)	4	G.O.C., Turkish	10
Forts, European (Turkish)	4	Gibraltar	27
Foulon, Colonel	21	Gough-Calthorpe, C.-in-C. Mediterranean,	
France	1,3,8,13,16,17,28	Vice-Admiral Hon. Sir Somerset A.	1,2,6,
Franchet d'Espérey, Général, Commander		Goulon, Colonel	7
Allied Armies in the Orient		Government, French	5,7
	2,3,6,11,13	Government, Hellenic (Greek)	13,25
Franklin-Bouillon, Monsieur, President,		Government, H.M. (British)	
French Senate	25,27	1,4,7,13,20,25,26	
Franks, Major-General George McK.		Government, German	6 fn
	21,22,23	Government, Italian	7
Fraternization	4	Government, Turkish Ottoman	
French	9,12,13,19,21,22,24,25	1,2,3,4,5,6,9,10,12,13,17,20,23,24 fn	
French Zone	8	Government, Turkish Republican	
Frontiers, Turkish-Bulgarian	28	(Nationalist)	1,27,28
Frontiers, Turkish-Greek	28	Government, Spanish	1
Fuller, Br.-General F.G.	7	Grand Vizier	10,11
		Great Britain	1,8
Galata	8,14	Greece	8,16,27,29
Gallipoli	11,19,26,27	Greeks	9,10,16,17,19,21,23 fn, 24,25
Gallipoli Peninsula	4,5,8,28		
Gargalides, General	14	Haidar Pasha	4,9,12,13,15,27
Garrison, International	17	Harbour Board	16
Garrison, Turkish	17	Harington, General Sir Charles	
Garrisons, Bosphorus	6	8,13,18,20,21,22,25,26,27,28,	
Garrisons, Dardanelles	6	Hedjaz	2,15

INDEX

Heywood, Lieut.-Colonel T.G.G.	22
Hospital, British Seamen	8
Hospital, No. 82 General	8
Hospitality (Turkish)	4
Hungary	6
Imbros	16
Ironside, Major-General Sir Edmund	13,14
Ismet Pasha	27
Ismid	9,10,11,12,14,17,24,25,227,28
Ismid Front	14
Ismid, Gulf of	15
Ismid Lines	13,14
Ismid Peninsula	9,13,20,24,28
Italian	9,12,13,20
Italy	1,8,16,17
Japan	16
Kadikeui	15
Kaiser, The German	20
Karabekir, General Kiazim	9
Kelly, Rear-Admiral John	26
Kemal, General Mustapha (Pasha)	9,10,11,13,24,25,27
Kemalists	24
Khartoum	28 fn
Konia	9
Kuchuk	15
Kut	1
Langlade, Colonel de	4
League of Nations	8,22
Lemnos	16
Liaison Section	23,24
Liaison Section, Inter-Allied	23
Lloyd George Mr. David	26
London	1,5,6,19 fn
Macedonia	3
Madrid	1
Mahdi	28 fn
Maitland Wilson, Lieut.-General Sir Henry F.	3,4,6,7,8,11,12,14,19
Malta	11,12,26
Maltepe	13
Marakis, General	27
Marden, Major-General Sir Thomas	19,23 fn, 26,27, 27 fn
Maritsa River	3,28
Maritza	27
Marmora, Sea of	11,14,15,16,27
Marseilles	25
Marshall, General Sir William	2
Mashlak	15
Medical School, Haidar Pasha	9
Medina	5
Mediterranean Stations	26
Mesopotamia	1,2,16,17
Mesopotamia Expeditionary Force	5
Millingon, Major O.H. van	12
Milne, General Sir George, Commander-in-Chief of the British Salonika Army	2,3,5 fn,6,7,8,9,10,12,13,14,17,18
Minister of Marine, Turkish (Ottoman)	10
Minister of War, Turkish (Ottoman)	4,10,11,13,23,24
Ministers, Hostile Turkish	12
Ministry of Supplies, Turkish (Ottoman)	2
Ministry of War, Turkish (Ottoman)	12
Mission, British	1
Mitylene	1
Mombelli, General	22,25,27
Montague-Bates, Br.-General F.S.	12
Mudania	9
Mudros, Lemnos	1
Munitions, Turkish	14
Mustapha Pasha	3
Mytilene	16
Nationals, Allied	29
Nationalist Bands	13, 13 fn,14
Nationalist Forces	12,27
Nationalist Movement	9,10,11,12,13,16,17,24 fn,25,26,28,29
Narrows, Dardanelles	26
Naval forces, Allied	6,12
North Bulair Lines	5

Occupation of the Rhineland 1918-29	5 fn
Officers, Allied Control	9
Officers, British	4,13
Officer's Club	7
Officers, Greek Venizelist	19
Offices of State, Turkish	12
Officials, Greek Civil	27
Ottoman	10
Ortakeui	6
Palace, Dolma Baghche	29
Palestine	1,16
Panderma	11
Pavlo	15
Peace Negotiations	1
Peace Proposals	1
Peace Terms	6 fn18
Pellé, General	21,28
Pera	4,7,14
Pera, English Girls School, Gande Rue	4
Pera, London Hotel	4
Pera, Military School	6
Pera, Palace Hotel	4
Persia, North	14
Plumer, Field-Marshal Lord, Governor of Malta	26
Poland	6
Police, Constantinople	6
Police, Organization	7
Police, Turkish	16
Powers, Allied	16
President, Inter-Allied Military Commission of Control	20
President of the United States of America (Wilson, Woodrow)	1
Prime Minister, Greek	19
Prisoners of War, British	23 fn,29
Prisoners of War, Turkish	23 fn
Pro-German Turkish Cabinet	1
Propaganda (Turkish)	4
Punjabis	11
Railway, Anatolian	4,8,12,13,17

Railway, Anatolian line	8
Railway, Baghdad	8
Railway, Mudania–Brusa	8
Railway, Oriental (in Europe)	8
Railway, Ottoman Anatolian	8
Railway, Ottoman Aidin (Smyrna)	8
Railway, Ottoman Aidin, Smyrna-Aidin line	8
Railway, Smyrna-Cassaba & Extension	8
Railways	2
Railways, British Director of	8
Railways, Ottoman Empire	8
Refugees, Russian	19
Report, Intelligence	9
Representative, Turkish	1
Resources, Turkey	16
Rhineland	17
Rhodes, Br.-General G.B.	9
Robeck, Admiral Sir John de	7
Rolland, Lieut.-Colonel C.E.T.	12
Royalists, Greek	19
Rumania	16
Rumbold, Sir Horace, Bart.	18,28
Russia	16
Russians, White	5,19
Sakaria River	25
Salonika	1,3,4,9
Samothrace	16
Sanders General Liman von	4
San Stefano	4
Sarriyanis, Colonel	27
Scutari	7,12,14,19,26
Sèvres, Treaty of	8
Shuttleworth, Br.-General D.I.	12,26
Sileh	15
Sivas	10
Slatin Pasha, Major-General Sir Rudolph	28 fn
Smyrna	6,9,10,16,17,24,28
Smyrna Zone	13
Special Elements, Turkish	16,21
Solly-Flood, Br,-General R.E.	10
Sopwith Snipe	26

INDEX

Sovereignty, Turkish Rights of	16	Troops, American	1
Stambul	3,4,7,8,10,14	Troops, Arab	1
Straits, The	16,17,18	Troops, Austrian	4
Straits, Zone Of The	16,17,18,28	Troops, Belgian	1
Struggle, Turkish-Greek	24	Troops, British	1,3,5,12,23 fn,25
Sub-Commission, Control	21	Troops, French	1,11,13,25,26
Sub-Commission, Control of Disarmament	23	Troops, French Reinforcements	25
		Troops, Germans	4
Sub-Commission, Disarmament	21,22,23	Troops, Hellenic (Greek)	19,20,25,27
Sub-Commission, Gendarmerie	21,23	Troops, Italian	13,26
Sub-Commission, Organization	21	Troops, Turkish Ottoman	4,5,12
Sub-Commission, Special Elements	23	Troops, Turkish Nationalist	13,25,27,28
Subjects, British	7	Turkey	1,5,6,8,10,11,16,17,22,27,28,29
Subjects, French	7	Turkish Provinces	10
Subjects, German	7	Turkish Republic	28
Subjects, Greek	7	Turks	1,6,8,11,13,16,17,20,21,23, fn,24,25,26,27,28,29
Subjects, Hellenic	7		
Subjects, Inter-Allied	7	Tuzla	15
Subjects, Italian	7		
Subjects, Poles	7	United Kingdom	9,26,27
Subjects, Rumanians	7	U.S.A.	8,16
Subjects, Russian	7		
Subjects, Turkish	7	Venizelos	19,29
Sultan (Turkish)	4,28	Versailles	1,3,6,8,19
Supreme Council	8		
Syria	2,5,13 fn,16	Waldersee, Field-Marshal Graf	19
		War graves	29
Talaat Pasha, Grand Vizier	1	War memorials	29
Territory, Turkish	28	War Office, British	1,3,10,12,18,19 fn, 21 fn,22,23,25,26
Tigris	1		
Therapia	15	War Office, Turkish Ottoman	23,24
Thrace	6,10,13,17,25,27,28	Western Front	1
Threat, Greek	25	Wilson, General Sir Henry G.I.C.S.	19 fn
Topart, Général	3	Wingate, General Francis	2
Townshend, Major-General Sir Charles	1	Wrangel, General A.	19
Transcaucasia	10		
Treaty, Italo-Turkey	24 fn	Y.M.C.A.	7
Treaty, Peace	13,19,20		
Treaty With Germany, Peace	8,16		
Treaty Of Lausanne, Peace	28		
Treaty Of Lausanne, Articles	28		
Treaty Of Sèvres, Peace	16,17,23,24,28		
Treasury, Turkish	16		
Troops, Allied	6,12,13,20,28		

INDEX TO ARMS, FORMATIONS AND UNITS

Army, Anglo-Egyptian	28 fn	Regiment, 20th Hussars	12,15
Army of the Black Sea	6,7,12,18	Regiment, 29th Hussars	13
Army of the Danube	43 fn,5	Regiment, Irish Guards	26
Army, Greek	6,17,20	Regiment, 9/King's Own	5 fn
Army, Turkish	2,24,28	Regiment, 1/K.O.S.B.	26
Nationalist	24	Regiment, 1/Loyal Regiment	26
Army of Occupation	16,17,19,29	Regiment, 3/Middlesex	4
Army of the Orient (Allied)	11	Regiment, Royal Engineers	18
Battalions, Guards	27	26th Field Company.	13
Corps, XII	3	Regiment, 2/R. Sussex	26
Corps, Greek I.	3	Regiment, 2nd/Sherwood Foresters	26
Division, 22nd	3, 5 fn	Regiment, 9/South Lancashire	5 fn
Division, 26th	3, 5 fn	Regiment, 1/South Staffordshire	27
Division, 27th	5,10	Regiment, French 45th	4
Division, 28th	3, 5 fn,10 fn,22,17	Regiment, French 84th	4
Division, French 122nd	11,20	Regiment, French 148th	4
Brigade, Guards	26	Regiment, Italian III/62nd	4
Brigade, R.F.A. Egypt	26	Regiment, French African Tirailleurs	15
Brigade, Medium R.F.A.	26	Regiment, French Moroccan Spahis	15
Brigade, XVII R.F.A.	26	Regiment, French Senegalese Tirailleurs	15
Brigade, V Pack R.F.A.	26	Regiment, 16th Greek Infantry	13
Brigade, 80th	10	R.A.F. "Q" Force	13,18,27
Brigade, 81st	10	No. 4 Squadron	26
Brigade, 82nd	10	No. 25 Squadron	26
Brigade, 83rd	4,6,12,26,27	No. 55 Squadron	13
Brigade, 84th	4,6,27	No. 56 Squadron	26
Brigade, 85th	4,14,27	No. 207 Squadron	26
Brigade, 242nd	12,13,14,17	No. 208 Squadron	26
Regiment, 3/Coldstream Guards	26	Royal Marines	26
Regiment, 1/Duke of Wellington	27	Royal Navy	8,12,26,27
Regiment, 9/East Lancashire	5 fn	Atlantic fleet	27
Regiment, 2/East Surrey	15	Mediterranean fleet	27
Regiment, 1/Gordon Highlanders	13,26	H.M.S. Agamemnon	2
Regiment, 2/Grenadier Guards	26	H.M.S. Ramillies	13
Regiment, 2/Highland L.I.,	26	Navy, Greek Fleet	21
Regiment, 3rd Hussars	26	Navy, Turkish	16

www.ingramcontent.com/pod-product-compliance
Ingram Content Group UK Ltd.
Pitfield, Milton Keynes, MK11 3LW, UK
UKHW021256180426
11947UKWH00011B/815